The Challenge of Diversity
Involvement or Alienation in the Academy?

by Daryl G. Smith

ASHE-ERIC Higher Education Report 5, 1989

Prepared by

Clearinghouse on Higher Education
The George Washington University

In cooperation with

Association for the Study
of Higher Education

Published by

School of Education and Human Development
The George Washington University

Jonathan D. Fife, Series Editor

Cite as
Smith, Daryl G. *The Challenge of Diversity: Involvement or Alienation in the Academy?* Report No. 5. Washington, D.C.: School of Education and Human Development, The George Washington University, 1989.

Library of Congress Catalog Card Number 89-63437
ISSN 0884-0040
ISBN 0-9623882-5-4

Managing Editor: Christopher Rigaux
Manuscript Editor: Barbara Fishel/Editech
Cover design by Michael David Brown, Rockville, Maryland

The ERIC Clearinghouse on Higher Education invites individuals to submit proposals for writing monographs for the *ASHE-ERIC Higher Education Report* series. Proposals must include:
1. A detailed manuscript proposal of not more than five pages.
2. A chapter-by-chapter outline.
3. A 75-word summary to be used by several review committees for the initial screening and rating of each proposal.
4. A vita and a writing sample.

ERIC Clearinghouse on Higher Education
School of Education and Human Development
The George Washington University
One Dupont Circle, Suite 630
Washington, DC 20036-1183

This publication was prepared partially with funding from the Office of Educational Research and Improvement, U.S. Department of Education, under contract no. ED RI-88-062014. The opinions expressed in this report do not necessarily reflect the positions or policies of OERI or the Department.

EXECUTIVE SUMMARY

For years, researchers have forecast the increasing diversification of students in higher education as a result of changing demographics and a variety of other social and economic shifts. The diverse elements of today's student body include age, gender, ethnic and racial backgrounds, and increasing numbers of differently abled and part-time students. Despite the difficulties inherent in generalizing across such disparate groups and individuals, the issues higher education faces fundamentally relate to the capacity of institutions to function in a pluralistic environment. While it is unrealistic to assume that higher education will solve all these challenges independent of the rest of society, it is clear that the successful involvement of diverse populations has significant implications for education and for the nation.

What Is the Current Status of Enrollments, Graduation Rates, and the Campus Climate?

Although the makeup of today's student bodies is more diverse than 20 years ago, current enrollments suggest that this trend has reversed itself for some groups. Moreover, many students are clustered not only in segments of the post-secondary system but also in various levels and fields. Several recent national reports have sounded an alarm that the progress with respect to enrollments is not sufficient. Observers generally agree that retention overall and the retention rate for certain specific populations are critical problems for many institutions, even though surprisingly little is known about retention for most minority populations and for other non-traditional groups. One of the more troubling themes to emerge is that many campuses do not effectively involve students who are different. Students must confront stereotypic attitudes, unfamiliar values, ineffective teaching methods, and an organizational approach that may not support their efforts to succeed. While such concerns are prominent in the experience of minority students, issues of stereotyping, social isolation, and alienation are found in each of the literatures on women, disabled students, and adult learners as well. Indeed, in contemporary higher education, the condition of diversity is all too often a condition of alienation. Given these institutional patterns, the dominant focus on the preparation of students as the primary issue appears to be overemphasized. The questionable validity of many instruments used to predict performance and the evidence of other factors affecting performance suggest that other characteristics of students and noncognitive measures and more critically, the institutional role in student success, need to be considered.

What Theoretical Perspectives Might Be Useful?
The literatures on involvement, cultural pluralism, intergroup relations, and demography illuminate some of the issues present today on many campuses and provide a perspective that might be helpful in addressing them. Considerable theoretical and research evidence supports the importance of students' involvement and integration. Such evidence points to the need for increased opportunities for cooperative learning and significant interactions among peers and with faculty. The literature on intergroup relations suggests, however, tinvolvemente involvement cannot be achieved simply by putting people together. The quality of the environment, power relationships, degree of competition, levels of frustration, and institutional support all contribute to the quality of interaction and relationships. Furthermore, the literature on cultural pluralism suggests that the current notion of simply respecting differences is an oversimplification that avoids concerns about genuine differences in values and approaches and the ways in which institutional values also must change. The literature on demography indicates that as long as some groups are underrepresented, the experience of tokenism—including isolation and heightened visibility—will emerge. One of the greatest challenges of diversity rests on integrating the objectives of involvement into the fabric of pluralism.

What Are the Patterns in Institutions Labeled Successful?
Five major themes emerge from a variety of studies looking at successful institutions. These institutions:

1. Focus on students' success and provide the tools for success;
2. Have begun to develop programs for increased coordination with elementary and secondary grades and for enhanced articulation between community colleges and four-year colleges and universities;
3. Dedicate energy and resources to creating an accepting environment that nourishes and encourages success;
4. Have access to good information that focuses on the insti-

tution and students;
5. Include leaders in the faculty and administration who provide strong direction for these efforts.

In addition to the insights that can be developed from successful institutions, lessons can be learned from women's colleges and from historically black institutions. Despite notable challenges to their survival, these institutions have contributed significantly to the success of women and to African-American students, particularly in that they provide an environment that believes in the potential and success of their students and involves them in all aspects of the institution. Central to their success is the presence of many African-American and female faculty and administrators.

What Are the Fundamental Issues of Organizing for Diversity?

The basic conceptual framework for many of the more traditional responses to diversity has focused essentially on *student assistance*. These approaches address the particular needs or "problems" felt to be barriers to students' success. Many institutions have broadened these efforts to include *institutional accommodations,* which acknowledges that some of the barriers to success rest with the institution itself. While these accommodations are steps in the right direction, they are not sufficient in themselves. They should be viewed as part of a broader effort included in the capacity of institutions to *organize for diversity.* At the core of this effort will be an organization's ability to educate in a pluralistic society for a pluralistic world. To reach such a place requires a shift not only in thinking but also in framing the questions we ask. The challenges of such fundamental transformation mean grappling with a number of complex issues:

- *Diversity of faculty and staff.* Diverse perspectives are required to develop organizations sensitive to pluralism. Despite overwhelming agreement that diversity in faculty and staff is essential for all institutions, the goal may prove difficult. The lack of growth in enrollments and the absence of students from nontraditional groups in the educational pipeline—particularly at the graduate and professional levels—threaten institutional goals for hiring women and minorities. Barriers to this effort are not only in a perceived lack of available candidates: A serious question exists as to whether institutions are promoting and retaining faculty members from nontraditional groups already present. Efforts to retain and promote from within are as important as increasing the pool of applicants.

- *Mission and values.* The issue of values emerges at a number of levels. Perhaps the most challenging has to do with the ways in which students perceive that the values and perspectives they bring are not appreciated and may even put them in conflict with the institution's norms and behaviors. Cooperation/conflict and individualism/community are two value domains where preferred modes of relating and learning may conflict with dominant institutional values. Institutions need to reflect on some of these values and on whether the institution is promoting assimilation rather than pluralism. Institutions must be very clear in differentiating between those values and goals that facilitate learning and the mission of the institution itself, and those values that leave individuals and groups relegated to the margin.

- *Educating for diversity.* Ignorance and insensitivity are commonly present on campuses, but institutions are beginning to articulate a commitment to educate all students and other members of the community for living in a pluralistic world. The content of the curriculum, styles of teaching, and modes of assessment are three elements in this effort.

- *Dealing with conflict.* The conditions for conflict are present on many campuses. Indeed, conflict may be an essential part of the process institutions will experience to clarify the many complex issues involved in creating pluralistic communities. Conflict may be part of the institutional learning process.

- *The quality of interaction.* A growing body of research evidence reflects the importance of students' involvement with the institution and peers and between students and faculty. While we know much less about the nature of this dynamic for many nontraditional groups, the quality of interaction, the attitudes of faculty, staff, and students toward one another, and the perception of the climate on campus must be evaluated and addressed.

- *The perceived conflict between quality and diversity.* The continuing message that a fundamental conflict exists between diversity and quality is perhaps the most compelling argument for reshaping the questions and the discourse about this topic. We *can* broaden our understanding about quality without diluting expectations for learning or for the curriculum, but to do so will require reframing our understanding about the meaning of quality, the definition of standards, performance criteria, and assessment. Many current approaches to assessment of students, programs, or faculty tend to devalue the performance of those who are different. Particular attention must be paid to the role of standardized testing and the increasing alarm about its validity for many nontraditional populations.

What Are the Implications of the Challenge of Diversity?

The challenge of diversity is national in scope. Given the complexities involved, no recipes are available to create truly pluralistic organizations. Institutions and policy makers can take some steps, however, to facilitate the process of adequately responding to diversity.

1. A comprehensive institutional assessment can provide important data from which priorities can be identified.
2. Cross-institutional research can identify successful institutions, identify ways in which involvement can be promoted, and clarify often conflicting material in the literature.
3. Coordination among the educational sectors can improve articulation and movement between levels and types of institutions.
4. Developing programs and funds can increase the number of students who enter teaching at all levels.
5. Organizations that succeed in meeting this challenge can also play a significant role in educating all future teachers and citizens to function in a diverse culture.
6. Providing increased local, state, and national financial aid will make access more possible for virtually every population of students.
7. Sustained commitment and effort rather than episodic interest will be required.
8. Leadership plays a central role, not only in setting goals and providing resources but also in framing the questions and setting the tone for deliberations.

If a single lesson is to be learned from the literature on diversity, it is that we cannot simply "add and stir." The challenges are many, but it is clear that the process of meeting them will bring great benefits to all members of the community and to the institution itself. The resources of diversity within an organization are more likely to prepare it for the future than any other resource.

ADVISORY BOARD

Roger G. Baldwin
Assistant Professor of Education
College of William and Mary

Carol M. Boyer
Consultant and Senior Academic Planner
Massachusetts Board of Regents of Higher Education

Ellen Earle Chaffee
Associate Commissioner of Academic Affairs
North Dakota State Board of Higher Education

Martin Finkelstein
Associate Professor of Higher Education Administration
Seton Hall University

Carol Everly Floyd
Associate Vice Chancellor for Academic Affairs
Board of Regents of the Regency Universities System
State of Illinois

George D. Kuh
Professor of Higher Education
Indiana University

Yvonna S. Lincoln
Associate Professor of Higher Education
University of Kansas

Michael A. Olivas
Professor of Law
University of Houston

Richard F. Wilson
Associate Chancellor
University of Illinios

Ami Zusman
Principal Analyst, Academic Affairs
University of California

CONSULTING EDITORS

Louis W. Bender
Director, State and Regional Higher Education Center
Florida State University

L. Leon Campbell
Provost and Vice President for Academic Affairs
University of Delaware

Darrell Clowes
Associate Professor of Education
Viginia Tech

Susan Cohen
Associate, Project for Collaborative Learning
Lesley College

John W. Creswell
Professor and Lilly Project Director
University of Nebraska

Andre Deruyttere
Vice President
Catholic University at Leuven, Belgium

Mary E. Dilworh
Director, Research and Information Services
ERIC Clearinghouse on Teacher Education

Lawrence Erickson
Professor and Coordinator of Reading and Language Studies
Southern Illinois University

J. Wade Gilley
Senior Vice President
George Mason University

Kenneth C. Green
Associate Director
Higher Education Research Institute
University of California at Los Angeles

Milton Greenberg
Provost
American University

Judith Dozier Hackman
Associate Dean
Yale University

John E. Roueche
Professor and Director, Community College Leadership Program
Sid W. Richardson Regents Chair
University of Texas

Mary Ellen Sheridan
Director of Sponsored Programs Administration
Ohio State University

William F. Stier, Jr.
Professor and Director of Intercollegiate Athletics
State University of New York at Brockport

Betty Taylor
Coordinator, Office of Educational Policy
New Jersey Department of Higher Education

Reginald Wilson
Senior Scholar
American Council on Education

CONTENTS

FOREWORD

Why should higher education be concerned with diversity?
This is more than just a rhetorical question. In the past several
years, a number of events has occurred that indicate that
higher education should *not* be concerned with diversity.
For example:

- Certain segments of the assessment movement have suggested that it is not the responsibility of higher education
  to rectify the acaemic weaknesses of secondary
  institutions.
- Education leaders, such as former Secretary of Education
  William Bennett, have called for a greater emphasis on
  academic studies stressing Western civilization. This type
  of emphasis sends a symbolic message that the history
  and culture of the non-Caucasian world does not matter.
- During the Reagan Administration there was a decrease
  of funds in constant dollar terms available for student
  financial aid. This sends a message that one must be both
  academically *and* economically qualified to obtain the
  advantage of higher education.
- Enforcement by the federal government of section 504
  to insure proper access for the otherwise abled has nearly
  ceased.

Four facts seem to be undeniable. First, the percentage
of minorities in the population is increasing at a significant
rate; second, college is increasingly the ticket to good jobs,
good life, and social and political influence; third, the enrollment of African-American males has decreased at both the
undergraduate and graduate level; and finally, when the
majority of a population feels disenfranchised from economic
parity and political influence then there is a high probability
of social instability.

Therefore, higher education's concern over the diversity
of its student and faculty is more than an academic discussion.
The recent evidence that indicate higher education's lack of
concern with diversity needs to be reversed. The first step
would be to heighten the consciousness of the entire academy
with the issues surrounding diversity. This report shows how
this can be accomplished. Daryl Smith, a professor of both
psychology and education at the Claremont Graduate School,
explains how diversifying a population is more than just a
matter of access. The entire structure of the organization must

be examined carefully for intentional or accidental bias and prejudice.

When an institution as a whole better understands the importance of the diversity issue, then diversity will cease having its polarizing effects. It does not have to be a liberal v. conservative objective. It should not be a egalitarian v. elitist goal. It should only be a social goal or a common goal for everyone who values a stable and just society.

Jonathan D. Fife
Professor and Director
ERIC Clearinghouse on Higher Education
School of Education and Human Development
The George Washington University

ACKNOWLEDGMENTS

I am grateful to many people who were helpful and supportive in the development of this monograph. Numbers of students and colleagues took the time to evaluate the manuscript and to assist me in the development of the ideas for this topic. Fay Rulau and Jane Gray were patient and diligent in the preparations of the document, and without the support and editorial suggestions of Barbara Bergmann, it would read with much less clarity. The anonymous reviewers were invaluable in their suggestions, and the staff at the ERIC Clearinghouse on Higher Education were always there to provide whatever guidance and support I needed.

I especially wish to acknowledge the work of many scholars whose material has not been published by mainstream presses and journals but whose work provided support and insight into the many complex challenges involved in addressing the topic of diversity. Their relative invisibility is symbolic of the problems inherent in this topic. Their work is very important.

Finally, I wish to salute the many administrators, faculty members, and students who are currently engaged in trying to meet the challenges of diversity through the transformation of their institutions. I hope that this report supports their efforts and provides an impetus for further action.

INTRODUCTION

For years, researchers have forecast the increasing diversification of students in higher education as a result of changing demographics and a variety of other societal and economic shifts (Frances 1980; Hodgkinson 1985). Indeed, dramatic changes have taken place in the composition of student bodies in American higher education. The diverse elements of today's student body include age, ethnic background, sexual preference, and ever-increasing numbers of "differently" abled, part-time, international, and commuting students. Despite the difficulties inherent in generalizing across such disparate groups and individuals, this report suggests that the issue higher education is facing fundamentally relate to the capacity of institutions to function in a pluralistic environment. In this context, the report addresses the changes in demographics that have taken place and raises some of the critical issues that emerge in responding to the challenge of diversity.

The theme of alienation ... is a powerful voice in the literature concerning racial and ethnic minorities.

Historically, as institutions have evaluated their success with different groups of students, most of the questions have focused on success in terms of the student and attributed success or failure to the student's background characteristics. Out of that research came a wealth of information on students' background characteristics, personality factors, and family origins and the relationship between those characteristics and academic success. While a rationale exists for this approach, the result has been that the problems and the responsibility to be successful were defined in terms of the individual. An extensive literature now suggests, however, that the issues facing nontraditional students go beyond their individual or group backgrounds—and even beyond the particular interaction of their background with the institutional environment—directly to the question of whether institutions are designed to deal with diversity. The theme of alienation pervades the literature. It is a powerful voice in the literature concerning racial and ethnic minorities. It is also present in the literature focusing on women, the disabled, and other nontraditional groups. A synthesis of this literature suggests that our research, programs, and institutional and public policy must be focused not only on the "needs" of each nontraditional group but also on the organizational issues institutions must address (Boyd 1982; Burrell 1980; Jaramillo 1988; Lunneborg and Lunneborg 1985; Pearson, Shavlik, and Touchton 1989; Verdugo 1986; Wilkerson 1987; Zambrana 1987).

In light of the broad literature describing the experiences

of many of these student groups, one of the central questions that emerges is how higher education will meet the challenge of diversity. Not enough progress has been made; indeed, in a number of areas it has been reversed. Although an alarm has been sounded, the calls to action may not yet adequately address the complexity and depth of the issues involved. By looking at many of the groups that have been at the margin of institutions of higher education, this monograph attempts to examine some of the critical issues that develop when an institution addresses the challenge of diversity.

It must be noted at the outset that the challenge of diversity is not new to this decade, to higher education, or to this country (Anderson 1987; Peterson et al. 1978). Indeed, since its founding, the United States has been viewed as a major social experiment precisely because of its efforts to create a single society involving people of diverse ethnic, religious, and national backgrounds. Traditionally, the metaphor for such an effort has been the "melting pot" in which people come from all over and create a new American culture. That image has increasingly been called into question. At its most basic, today's challenge calls for the creation of a society in which individual differences are respected and allowed to coexist. While such a statement is easy to make and to support, the *form* of that society is not very clear while the challenges of creating it are very real. The process of creating communities requires decisions and interactions that address fundamental values, preferences, or rights, some of which may conflict. Such decisions are also affected by levels of communication, styles of interaction, or perceptions about others that are related to a person's background. They are, in other words, strongly affected by diversity. Thus, the consequences of heterogeneity have dramatic implications at all levels of society and at all levels of the organizations within that society.

Clearly, we have not yet achieved a vision of what a pluralistic community should look like. Indeed, it is not clear that we even agree on all the elements of that vision. Volumes have been written addressing these questions: *The Negro in the United States* (Frazier 1957), *An American Dilemma* (Myrdal 1962), *The Nature of Prejudice* (Allport 1954), and "New Black-White Patterns" (Pettigrew 1985) are examples of such scholarship. It is therefore unrealistic to assume that higher education can on its own achieve pluralistic communities that do not reflect the problems in the larger society or that higher education can, independent of other institutions, solve all the challenges of diversity. But just as the issues of a culturally pluralistic society must be high on the national agenda, so too must they be high on the agendas of colleges and universities across the country. Not only will the successful involvement of diverse populations tip the balance between institutional survival and failure and between educational quality and mediocrity, but, more significantly, the social implications spread far beyond the academy.

Numerous national reports concerned in particular about the participation of minorities in higher education have articulated eloquent appeals for national and educational attention to this issue. One of the most recent, *One-Third of a Nation* (Commission on Minority Participation 1988), is a joint undertaking of the American Council on Education and the Education Commission of the States. It sounds a warning:

America is moving backward—not forward—in its efforts to achieve the full participation of minority citizens in the life and prosperity of the nation. . . . If we allow these disparities to continue, the United States will inevitably suffer a compromised quality of life and a lower standard of living (p. 1).

Most scholars tend to mark the late 1960s as the beginning of the changes in diversity in higher education. It is important to recognize, however, that colleges and universities have been adjusting to and accommodating "new" kinds of students almost since their founding. Although their efforts are most notable for their lack of success, attempts to educate Native Americans were part of the founding principles of a number of colonial colleges (LaCounta 1987). The move toward coeducation in the late 19th and early 20th centuries and the introduction of older students with the passage of the GI Bill following World War II provide examples of a broadening diversity in the populations that entered the academy before the sixties (Lasser 1987; Wilson 1987b). While ways in which students and institutions accommodated the new arrivals can be cited in each case, the need for changes that never occurred is more evident.

Earlier efforts to achieve diversity notwithstanding, the past two decades have witnessed a dramatic shift in the demographic makeup of society as a whole as well as an influx of new students in higher education that are more diverse than ever before. As such, the past 20 years have presented a challenge to American higher education that is deeper and more significant than any changes that preceded them.

Caveats

This monograph focuses on the challenges of diversity facing colleges and universities today. To attempt such a task, however, first requires a recognition of some of the limitations inherent in the process, including the ability to generalize and the limits of language.

The risk always exists that in attempting to address the broader issues of diversity, as this monograph does, the perspective of particular groups will become so generalized as to be unrecognizable. The reality is that important differences exist in the issues, histories, and experiences of specific groups of students—women, racial and ethnic minorities, the disabled. Certainly, the issues of child care faced by a student who is also a single parent are experienced differently from a student dealing with racial discrimination (Pounds 1987). It will be suggested, however, that unless institutions come to grips with diversity and the issues related to it, it will be difficult to address specific issues brought by individual groups.

Researchers must always be prepared to struggle with the challenges presented by the need to summarize, to generalize, and to reach conclusions, while at the same time recognizing the distinctive experiences of particular groups. It is ironic that in stressing this distinctiveness, we are concurrently creating classifications that are quickly rendered inadequate. We classify people into groups by gender, age, minority, disability. We classify institutions as two-year colleges, research universities, private or public institutions. It quickly becomes apparent that these groupings are themselves too simplistic (Hughes 1983; Pounds l987).

Too often the definition of "handicap" conjures up the image of a wheelchair. The institutional response to the differently abled then is to build ramps, a modification of no consequence to someone who is deaf or learning disabled. Those with learning disabilities are an important part of this group yet have very different needs based not only on the handicap itself but also on the fact that this handicap is not visible (Schmidt and Sprandel 1982). The literature frequently describes the Latino population without recognizing that this group includes people from very diverse backgrounds whose experiences in colleges and universities are not at all uniform (Burgos-Sasscer 1987). The census classifies as "Hispanic" those of Mexican-American, Puerto Rican, Cuban, and Central or South American origin (Brown, Rosen, and Hill 1980). Of the 17.3 million people classified as Hispanic in 1985, over 10 million were Mexican-Americans and 2.6 million Puerto Ricans (McKenna and Ortiz 1988; Salganik and Maw 1987). Four hundred eighty-one tribes are classified as Native American, each with its own traditions yet each one sharing some part of the experience of being grouped together as one.

The Asian-American population is another important example of this issue. The classification "Asian-American" includes, among others, the experiences of those of Japanese, Chinese, Vietnamese, Cambodian, Korean, Philippine, and Pacific Island origins. While over 60 Asian-American subgroups are described in the literature (Carter, Pearson, and Shavlik 1988), much of the literature either categorizes all of these peoples together or discusses the experiences of just one or two of them, ignoring the rest. Sensitivity is expressed in the literature by those concerned about Asian-Americans. Asians are assumed to be an example of the "model" minority group that has made a successful transition to higher education, with their only issues being related to the burdens of overachievement and overenrollment. These assumptions ignore the wide variations among their subgroups and ignore the issues of racial discrimination, access, and success that do exist (Hsia 1987, 1988; Sue 1977, 1979).

By the same token, almost all the literature dealing with African-American populations, women, adults, and the disabled increasingly points to the need to acknowledge the very great differences in individuals and subgroups that exist. Gender, for example, provides an important division for every other subgroup. Women of color face invisibility when certain issues facing those in this group are ignored under discussions of race or gender.

Thus, the danger of overgeneralizing on the one hand and being so specific on the other makes it difficult to come to any conclusions. This danger is one that institutions and scholars of higher education must confront, as it represents one of the difficult challenges of diversity itself. Nevertheless, it is through the various literatures on specific groups that this monograph was developed. Clearly, it would be impossible to adequately review the separate literatures that now exist on the adult learner, the African-American student, the Latino student, the disabled student, and so on. It is not the intent of this monograph to do that. These literatures, however, are critical to the topic—and they have been reviewed to try to bring together the common themes that address diversity.

Another caveat involves the problem of language—a problem that takes two forms. The first is the question of how to describe the various groups being discussed in a way that respects their traditions and preferences. Our language is in constant flux, and it takes time for consensus to develop about the naming of groups. The once common use of such terms as "minority" and "black" has now shifted. In the meantime, choices have been made that attempt to respect current preferences. For example, this monograph uses the term "Latino" as the term of choice, despite the fact that the Census Bureau uses the term "Hispanic" for data collection. Despite the Census Bureau's classification of Native Americans as Native Americans, this monograph uses the former as the identification to be used, except when referring to population tables. References to physical and learning disabilities or impairments can be controversial. As those who are "differently abled" achieve a greater degree of visibility and power within society, efforts will no doubt continue to find a "label" that feels suitable (Duffy 1989). This monograph refers to those who are differently abled as the disabled because of the literature in this area. The issue of labels is important and significant and thus controversial.

Another nomenclature issue is reflected in the extreme sensitivity that certain words have to various readers. Racism—or institutional racism—is increasingly being "named" on campuses as one fundamental cause of the problems facing campuses today. Others resist using such terms because of the defensiveness they cause. Nevertheless, common use of the phrase "qualified women or minorities," for example, reveals many troubling assumptions. We do not usually say "qualified whites." One cannot ignore the role of racism, sexism, and homophobia as they affect institutional practice and students' experiences. The emphasis in this monograph is on illuminating some of the emerging issues that campuses need to address.

The literature on the topic of diversity is very uneven, both in its quality and in the topics under discussion. The vast majority of the early literature on diversity, for example, focused on African-American students (Myrdal 1962; Pettigrew 1985; White and Sedlacek 1987). Very little has been written to date on Cambodian, Vietnamese, or Korean students, although some important studies on different Asian groups are included in the literature on counseling and human services (Sue 1979, 1981). Surprisingly little research on Chicanos has been undertaken until recently (Webster 1984). What is written on the disabled tends to focus on program development, with much less available on the students themselves, their satisfaction and retention, or other issues (Jarrow 1987).

A final caveat: Such a complex topic as diversity inevitably raises questions and problems that few societies—let alone institutions—have solved to all groups' satisfaction. The process of evaluating success in particular creates its own challenges. To a disenfranchised person, *some* progress is not very comforting, while to an administrator trying to create change, some progress might be all that can be expected. This monograph attempts to look at the question of success with both these perspectives in mind.

Framing the Question

The last section addressed the importance of nomenclature for "how the problem is named involves alternative scenarios, each with its own facts, values, judgments, and emotions" (Edelman 1977, p. 29). This concept is not simply an abstract one: It is a central part of the thesis of this monograph and one of the most difficult challenges facing decision makers. For example, when retention is named as the student dropout rate, we imply a problem with the student (Jaramillo 1988). When we define retention as an institution's graduation rate, we focus on the institution. Furthermore, "as long as we condone the use of metaphors [that] conjure up a scenario of individual initiative and responsibility for educational failure, change will not occur" (Jaramillo 1988, p. 27). This issue is most important, because the definition of a problem can dramatically affect the solutions sought, which has particular implications for the education of minorities, where too often failure has been focused on the student and the student's background. But the issue can be found in the approach of institutions to virtually all groups on the margin. It is also reflected in the development of new curricular approaches where early efforts focused on the absence of women or minorities from the curriculum. As curricula have been transformed, entire new fields and questions have emerged that point out the deficits in the canon rather than the deficits in women and minorities (McIntosh 1989).

Despite theoretical models in higher education stressing that the outcomes of education are the result of complex interactions between the student and the institution, much of the literature, programs, and research have focused on the student and the characteristics of the student that lead to success. Framing the questions in this way deemphasizes organizational issues and organizational change (Willie and Edmonds 1978). Carefully framing the question is an essential element in meeting the challenge of diversity.

THE STATUS OF DIVERSITY

It is easier to talk about a desire to create a report card for higher education—to evaluate its success—than to actually do it. While some objective data are available, success also depends upon the choice of relevant criteria. This choice and the interpretation of the data vary depending upon the view one brings to the study. Moreover, it is difficult to imagine discussing higher education without reflecting the multidimensionality of the system. Great variation is present within the system on most any criterion. In evaluating the response to diversity, however, the three most common measures involve patterns of enrollment, retention through completion of degree programs, and the institutional climate. The following sections evaluate higher education as a system in these terms.

The proportion of African-American and Latino young adults who are currently going on to college has declined in the 1980s.

Enrollment

How successful has higher education been in achieving a system of open access to diverse populations? The answer to this question depends in part on the specific criteria of success one wishes to employ. Once again, framing the question becomes critical. One can compare factors to the distant past, to the recent past, to population demographics, and to an ideal of what "ought to be." A number of studies outline areas of progress, areas of decline, and areas of stagnation (e.g., Commission on Minority Participation 1988; Green 1989; Pettigrew 1985; Wilson 1987a). In many cases, the same statistic may reflect both progress and decline. How should these statistics, for example, be evaluated? *In 1940, 5 percent of whites and 1 percent of blacks were college graduates. In 1985, the figures were 20 percent and 11 percent, respectively* (Center for Education Statistics 1987). The gap between the two groups was greater in 1985, but the ratio of progress was faster for African-Americans than whites—improvement according to one criterion, greater distance according to the other. As Gunnar Myrdal suggested in 1962, the significance to Americans is often not some degree of change achieved but looking at the change in light of the general value of the American creed, the ideal. Nevertheless, the uneven distribution of diversity and the lack of progress, particularly with respect to some populations, is part of the concern expressed today.

Much of the early literature and research in higher education began from the assumption that the typical college student was white, was 18 to 24 years of age, lived in a residence

TABLE 1

Higher Education Enrollments by Age, Gender, and Attendance Status, 1975 and 1985
(000)

	1975		1985		
	No.	%	No.	%	Change
Total	11,185		12,247		+9
14–24 years	7,061	63	7,151	58	+1
Over 25 years	4,124	37	5,099	42	+24
Men	6,149	55	5,818	48	−5
Women	5,036	45	6,429	52	+28
Full time	6,841	61	7,075	58	+3
Part time	4,344	39	5,172	42	+19

Source: Center for Education Statistics 1987, p. 123.

TABLE 2

Higher Education Enrollments by Racial/Ethnic Group, 1976 and 1984
(000)

	1976		1984		
	No.	%	No.	%	Change
Total	10,986		12,163		+11
Hispanic	384	3.5	529	4.3	+38
White	9,076	82.6	9,767	80.3	+8
Black	1,033	9.4	1,070	8.8	+4
Asian/Pacific Island	198	1.8	382	3.1	+93
Native American	76	0.7	83	0.7	+9
International	219	2.0	332	2.7	+52

Source: Center for Education Statistics 1987, p. 152.

hall, attended college full time, and was more often male than female. While a tendency remains to address questions as if these descriptors were still true, one would have a difficult time justifying such a description today. Tables 1 and 2 provide data on the enrollment characteristics of today's students, both graduate and undergraduate.

In fall 1985, 42 percent of all students were over 25, 52 percent were women, and 42 percent attended part time (table 1). Women over 25 were 24 percent of all students enrolled in 1986 (O'Barr 1989). In addition, in 1984 approximately 17 percent were members of an ethnic minority and another 3 percent were international students (table 2).

The largest ethnic minority is African-American, which in 1984 accounted for 8.8 percent of the total enrollment in higher education (table 2). In that same year, African-Americans made up 10.9 percent of the general population 18 years and older (Center for Education Statistics 1986). Latinos were 4.3 percent of the enrollments in higher education, compared to 6.3 percent in the general population over 18. Asians were 3.1 percent compared to approximately 2 percent of the general population in 1980, and Native Americans accounted for less than 1 percent of the total enrollment and of the population in general (Carnegie Foundation 1987; Chew and Ogi 1987; Hsia 1987).

While few data are available on the number of disabled students in higher education, current data suggest that from 3 to 6 percent of entering freshman claim a physical disability of some sort (Astin, Green, and Korn 1987; Fichten 1986). It is more difficult to determine rates for learning disabilities given the problems of definition and the lack of systematic research on this topic in most national studies (Claxton and Murrell 1987; Kirchner and Simon 1984; Lopez and Clyde-Synder 1983; Perry 1981).

Taken as an aggregate, these figures represent a considerable change from 20 years ago. The number of African-American students has more than doubled, and the representation of women, adult learners, and part-time students has increased considerably (Bean and Metzner 1985; Blake 1987; Lee, Rotermund, and Bertselman 1985; Sedlacek and Webster 1978). Today's overall enrollment figures in higher education do more adequately represent the patterns in the general population than they once did. Most of the changes, however, occurred during the late sixties and early seventies and reflect major efforts at the national, state, and local levels. The growth of the community college system, the move to a highly nonresidential and commuter student population, extensive federal and state financial aid programs, special services, and programmatic and curricular changes resulted in new populations of students. In particular, many authors cite financial aid as a key element in the change, particularly for minority populations (Astin 1982; Bean and Metzner 1985; Brown, Rosen, and Hill 1980; Oliver and Etcheverry 1987; Ostar 1985; Stampen and Fenske 1988; SHEEO 1987).

Current and recent enrollment trends demonstrate that the thrust of those earlier changes has shifted. The progress in some cases has slowed and in others has been reversed. While Asian and Latino enrollments have increased both absolutely and as a percentage of the enrollment, African-American enrollments declined between 1980 and 1984 despite increases in the high school completion rates of each group (Blake 1987; Carnegie Foundation 1987). Indeed, while the absolute and relative number of Latinos has increased, the increase is simply a function of the greater numbers graduating from high school rather than a function of an increased percentage going on to college. The proportion of African-American and Latino young adults who are currently going on to college has declined in the 1980s (Carnegie Foundation 1987; de los Santos 1986; Wilson 1987a, 1988). The general conclusion from this literature is that Latinos and Native Americans are still very much underrepresented. While the overall numbers for Asian students appear to be strong, the variation among Asian groups leaves some groups still underrepresented (Asian-American Student Association 1984; Hsia 1988; SHEEO 1987). In this instance, serious underlying issues become masked by grouping into one mass populations that are in truth quite different.

It must be recognized that the pattern of increases and declines in persons of color varies considerably from institution to institution. A 1987 study, for example, shows that while 20 percent of campuses reported increases in African-American enrollments, 13 percent reported declines. The same is true for other ethnic groups, though many more campuses reported increases in Asian students (21 percent) than losses (7 percent) (El-Khawas 1987; Lee 1985).

While estimates of the disabled in the population vary, it appears that these students are still very underrepresented, although the absence of good information and basic definitions makes establishing a base of comparison very difficult (Asch 1984; Jarrow 1987; Marion and Iovacchini 1983; Perry 1981).

Distribution of student enrollments according to institutional type

The 3,000 institutions of higher education in this country have not been uniformly successful in achieving diversity as measured by student enrollments. Although historically African-American institutions still enroll a disproportionate share of African-American students in higher education, the great

TABLE 3

Total Enrollment by Race/Ethnicity of Student and Type of Institution, Fall 1984
(000)

	All Institutions	Public (% of Total)		Private (% of Total)	
	No.	4-year	2-year	4-year	2-year
White	9.767	43	34	21	2
Black	1,070	40	39	18	4
Hispanic	529	33	53	12	2
Asian	382	41	42	16	1
Native American	83	36	51	10	4
Nonresident alien	332	51	15	33	1

Source: Center for Education Statistics 1987, p. 153.

majority of African-American students now attend traditionally white institutions (Allen 1987; Livingston and Stewart 1987; Morris 1979; Wright 1984). Most Native American students are enrolled in approximately 20 primarily Native American colleges, most of which are community colleges (Fries 1987).

Table 3 illustrates the enrollment patterns for minority students between public and private institutions and between two- and four-year colleges and universities. Among all college students, 77 percent attend public institutions and about 35 percent attend two-year public institutions. For Latino students, the figures are 86 percent in public institutions and 53 percent in two-year public institutions, for Asians 83 percent and 42 percent, and for Native Americans 87 percent and 51 percent. The most striking pattern to note is the high percentage of Latino and Native American students attending public two-year institutions. Because of the generally lower transfer and completion rates for two-year colleges, these figures have implications for retention and the completion of the baccalaureate degree (Arciniega 1985; Mingle 1987; Richardson and Bender 1987; Turner 1987).

Table 4 was prepared as the result of evidence indicating it is important to look at the differences between public and private institutions as well as different levels of institutions—universities, four-year colleges, and two-year colleges (Clowes, Hinkle, and Smart 1986; Lee 1985; Morris 1979). This analysis separates the enrollment figures by level and by type of insti-

TABLE 4

Enrollment by Institutional Type and Race/Ethnicity, Fall 1984[a]

All Institutions	All	White	Black	Hispanic	Asian	Native American	Foreign
Universities	24%	25%	13%	13%	24%	15%	42%
4-year	39%	40%	44%	32%	32%	30%	42%
2-year	37%	36%	43%	54%	43%	55%	16%
Universities							
Public	18%	19%	9%	9%	17%	13%	28%
Private	6%	6%	4%	4%	7%	2%	14%
4-year colleges							
Public	25%	24%	30%	24%	24%	23%	22%
Private	14%	15%	14%	8%	9%	7%	20%
2-year colleges							
Public	35%	34%	39%	53%	43%	51%	15%
Private	2%	2%	4%	1%	1%	4%	1%

[a]Totals may not be 100 as a result of rounding.
Source: Center for Education Statistics 1987, p. 153

tution for students using fall 1984 enrollment figures. The data suggest that four-year institutions, particularly four-year *public* institutions, have the most even distribution of students across racial lines. While community colleges have a disproportionate share of minority enrollments, research universities have fewer minority members.

An alternative way to look at these figures is to compare minority distribution by type of institution. Table 5 illustrates that public four-year and public and private two-year institutions have the highest percentage of minority enrollments. The percentage of persons of color ranges from 24 percent in private two-year colleges to 15 percent in public universities. Once again, however, the pattern varies among ethnic groups. Latinos are most represented in public two-year institutions, African-Americans in private two-year and public four-year institutions.

The status of overall enrollment demographics over the last 10 years suggests improvement in numbers for Asian students as a group and for women but less improvement, even loss, for Latinos and African-Americans. It is also clear that students are clustered not only in various segments of the postsecondary system but also in various levels and fields within

TABLE 5

Institutional Profile by Racial Enrollment, Fall 1984[a]

Universities			4-Year		2-Year	
	Public	Private	Public	Private	Public	Private
Whites	85%	81%	79%	83%	78%	76%
Blacks	5	6	11	8	10	16
Hispanics	2	3	4	3	7	4
Asian	3	4	3	2	4	1
Native American	[b]	[b]	[b]	[b]	1	1
Foreign	4	6	2	4	1	1

[a]Totals may not be 100 as a result of rounding.
[b]Less than 1 percent.
Source: Center for Education Statistics 1987, p. 153.

higher education. For example, the representation of women in the sciences and engineering has improved but is still very low. Moreover, the underrepresentation of African-Americans, Latinos, and Native Americans in certain fields, such as the sciences, and at the graduate and professional levels is also apparent (Astin 1982; Blackwell 1988; Carnegie Foundation 1987; Dix 1987; Stern 1988; Trent 1984; Trent and Braddock 1988). In general, the literature cites the issue of uneven distribution in fields for all minorities and for women. This underrepresentation has significant implications for the future of higher education and for society.

Enrollment projections

Several possible scenarios can emerge from an analysis of the relationship between population demographics and patterns of college enrollment. One can assume, for example, that as the population in society diversifies, so too will the populations of colleges and universities. These projections are based on assumptions that the patterns of diversification will continue if only because the demographics of society are changing (Commission on Minority Participation 1988; Estrada 1988; Hodgkinson 1985; Wilson 1987a). Society is getting older, and more adults are expressing interest in furthering their education. Moreover, the ethnic makeup of precollegiate students reflects the increasingly diverse minority populations present in society. It is anticipated that by 2000, one-third of all school-age children will be members of ethnic minorities and that by 2010, one-third of the nation will be African-

American, Latino, Asian, or Native American (Commission on Minority Participation 1988; Lee 1985; Wilson 1987b). Latinos alone are the second-largest and fastest-growing minority population in the United States (White and Sedlacek 1987). Moreover, it is likely that the disabled college population will also continue to grow as more differently abled students graduate from high school and efforts are intensified to provide access and support for them (Asch 1984; California Community Colleges 1986; Fichten 1986; Hameister 1984; Health Resource Center 1987; Mick 1985).

For this view to hold, institutional matriculation and success rates for the various subgroups in the population would have to be roughly equivalent. It also assumes that once arriving at the university, success rates would be roughly equal. This scenario is implicit in our assumptions about a desirable future. Certainly a review of today's enrollment patterns would support the view that this scenario has taken place in many institutions *to some degree and in some places.* Yet in some very important ways, it is not occurring. Enrollment patterns will not change simply because the population has changed.

A second view would predict that the demographic makeup within higher education will not reflect the changing character of the population and that a significant education gap will occur among groups in society. This scenario could emerge for a variety of different reasons. Differences in high school completion rates, differences in perception about the value of higher education, differences in institutional performance could all create this long-term picture. It is also possible that different subgroups of the population will not view higher education as capable of meeting their goals and will choose alternative routes for advancement (Arbeiter 1987). The number of adults today attending alternative forms of postsecondary education and the larger number of minorities pursuing work and the military as alternatives to continued education give credence to this possibility (Cox and Jobe 1988; Wilson 1987b).

A third scenario would project dramatically uneven distributions of these various populations throughout postsecondary education, with some being educated at more selective colleges and universities and others being clustered in two-year institutions. While it may be the case that different institutions serve very different purposes and may thus serve certain populations better than others, distribution according to racial, gender, or age breakdowns raises serious questions for society. A policy analysis of the status of African-Americans in higher education cautions (along with many others) that access cannot simply be evaluated across all of higher education (Morris 1979). "Higher education in the United States has evolved into a highly refined institutional status hierarchy" (Astin, quoted in Morris 1979, p. 56).

These three scenarios are all possibilities and to some degree are reflected in today's statistics. Thus, to the degree that each scenario is true today, the conclusion concerning higher education's success in achieving diversity in its enrollments is mixed (Chacon, Cohen, and Strover 1986; El-Khawas 1987; Hill 1984; Richardson, Simmons, and de los Santos 1987). Part of the concern expressed in the literature relates to the consequences that each scenario has for society.

*In some way, our life as a nation depends both on culti-
vating intelligence to keep our complex social order running
and preventing the formation of a permanently alienated,
undereducated, unemployed, "under class"* (Bruner 1983,
p. 196).

Retention
Retention is an important measure of success, but it is complicated by a variety of definitions and by the variety of ways in which it is measured. Institutional retention, for example, is a very important measure of success for institutions but, from the standpoint of public policy, may be less critical than retention as measured by completion of a degree. The general conclusions about retention in the literature emerge from a number of different sources. Some researchers have looked at the national rate of degree completion compared to enrollment to estimate retention rates (Commission on Minority Participation 1988). Others have studied the retention rates of specific groups at the institutional level; still others have used such national data bases as the *Cooperative Institutional Research Project* or *High School and Beyond* to assess retention and degree completion (Hill 1984; Hilton 1986; Morris 1979; Tinto 1987). In general, the literature agrees that the overall retention of minorities, particularly African-Americans, Latinos, and Native Americans, is lower than retention for white students and that overall retention is now about equal for men and women (Nettles 1988b; SHEEO 1987). The data

on men and women overall and on men and women of color suggest that the timing of degree completion and the nature of the reasons when the degree is not completed differ (Tinto 1987). Little data exist on retention as a function of age, though some data indicate that older students and other non-traditional students are more apt to leave for reasons external to the institution, such as jobs and family considerations, than would be true for traditional students (Bean and Metzner 1985).

While most studies conclude that the rates of degree completion for African-Americans, Latinos, and Native Americans are below that of whites and that the number of degrees conferred to African-Americans has declined since 1975, the figures vary with the sample and measure being used (Blake 1987; Cardoza 1986; Commission on Minority Participation 1988; Council of Graduate Schools 1986; Hill 1984; Hilton 1986; Nettles 1988a; Sanders 1987; SHEEO 1987; Sudarkasa 1987; Webster 1984; Wilson 1987a, 1988). Nevertheless, many authors point with alarm to the dropout rates for these groups (Blake 1987; Commission on Minority Participation 1988; Sanders 1987; Wilson 1987a). One study estimates the rate of degree completion for whites to be two and one-half times the rate of degree completion for Latinos (Council of Graduate Schools 1986), while another reports that the dropout rate for Native Americans is between 75 and 93 percent (Guyette and Heth 1983). In any case, "a decline in educational attainment by any substantial population group is cause for deep concern" (Commission on Minority Participation 1988, p. 14).

Again, types of institutions vary considerably. Some have pointed to the success of historically African-American colleges and some of the more selective institutions in retaining and graduating minority students (Allen 1987; Blake 1987; Fleming 1984; Gurin and Epps 1975; Hart 1984; Morris 1979; Pascarella 1985; Tinto 1987). As stated earlier, historically African-American colleges continue to account for a greater proportion of undergraduate and advanced degrees awarded to African-Americans relative to the smaller proportion of African-American students now attending historically African-American colleges and universities (Hart 1984; Morris 1979; Nettles 1988a; Richardson, Simmons, and de los Santos 1987; Wilson 1988). Some caution, however, that the picture is mixed at African-American institutions (Nettles, Thoeny, and

Gosman 1986): Their recent studies have found that rates of progression are slower and rates of attrition are actually higher overall at African-American institutions than at white institutions. Significant here are the background differences of students in attendance and whether the institution is public or private (Hartnett 1970; Nettles 1988b). African-American institutions admit students who are less prepared by traditional standards and thus may be expected to have a higher rate of attrition. The data suggest that these institutions still graduate greater proportions of students than white institutions where the rate of attrition cannot be fully explained by academic preparation.

Some evidence also suggests that private institutions in general and African-American private institutions in particular are more successful with regard to retention (Davis and Nettles 1987; Hart 1984; Hill 1984; Nettles, Thoeny, and Gosman 1987). Indeed, the proportion of degrees awarded to minorities in private institutions is twice that of public institutions (Richardson, Simmons, and de los Santos 1987). These data are confounded by the heavy presence of minority students in public two-year institutions, where relatively few students move to four-year institutions (Chacon, Cohen, and Strover 1986). Clearly, care must be exercised in making simple conclusions across institutions and institutional types. The interactions of race, gender, and institutional type and control are significant and can affect general conclusions about retention (Pascarella 1985). Nevertheless, retention is a cause for national concern.

Achieving full integration concern[s] not only numbers but also treatment by faculty, attitudes on campus . . . curricula. . . harassment, the absence of role models, limited opportunities for leadership, and, even more fundamentally, approaches to learning.

The Campus Environment— ## A "Chilly Climate"

Many campuses today look very different from 20 years ago, and a cursory glance might suggest that higher education has made significant progress in terms of students' diversity. But the challenge of diversity goes beyond the kinds of changes evidenced by increased programs and services. The consistent theme of alienation experienced by students of nontraditional backgrounds in their campus environments is symptomatic of a deep underlying problem that has not been adequately addressed. The voices of these students are those of people who feel like outsiders, "strangers in a strange land" (Beckham 1988). The current literature suggests that some campus environments are more "chilly" than welcoming, more "alienating" than involving, more hostile than encouraging.

Again, it is important to recognize that generalizations across a complex and diverse system are risky. Information about students' experiences on their campuses, while significant, does not reflect the universal view of all students, nor does it reflect individual students' view of their campuses. One study of African-American students at predominantly white institutions reports, for example, that their experiences were "not very unpleasant or very pleasant" (Allen 1982), while a later work reports that experiences of racial discrimination were frequent (Allen 1986). These mixed conclusions are not uncommon and may be related to degrees of association and to such factors as social distance (Carter and Sedlacek 1984; Griffith 1978; Loo and Rolison 1986; Lunneborg and Lunneborg 1985; Patterson and Sedlacek 1984; Peterson et al. 1978).

Although it is important to keep this perspective in mind, the following comment should nevertheless cause the higher education community to pause and reflect:

> *If a Rip Van Winkle who retired in 1966 came back today, resumed his reading of the* Chronicle of Higher Education, *and browsed through . . .* Change, *he would have to wonder not at the magnitude of change since 1965 but at the continuity of problems. . . . The statistics for blacks are anything but cheering. . . . Yet perhaps the most conspicuous change a Rip would note is the deteriorated climate for interracial unity. . . . The presence of blacks in higher education falls woefully short of where men and women of good will hoped and trusted it would be by 1987* (Bornholdt 1987, pp. 6–7).

More sobering, this statement should not be read with only African-American students in mind, because it could apply to virtually all nontraditional populations in one way or another. The literature reviewed through the following sections cites a myriad of barriers facing the diversity of students on their campuses, barriers that can be psychosocial, academic, financial, and physical. All too frequently, it mentions alienation (Asamen and Berry 1987; Skinner and Richardson 1988; Vasquez 1982).

Women
The phrase "a chilly climate" was coined to reflect the experience of women on today's campuses for a report that says

women, even though they constitute a majority of students, have not become fully integrated on today's campuses (Sandler and Hall 1982). As other studies have suggested, the issues involved in women's achieving full integration concern not only numbers but also treatment by faculty, attitudes on campus about gender, curricula that still ignore the contributions of women, sexual harassment, the absence of role models, limited opportunities for leadership, and, even more fundamentally, approaches to learning that have not traditionally been reflected in the very value system of higher education (Belenky et al. 1986; Pearson, Shavlik, and Touchton 1989; Sandler 1987; Walton 1986). Such research suggests that varieties of approaches to learning and inclinations toward cooperative learning styles, for example, are not easily accommodated on many campuses (Claxton and Murrell 1987; Rossi 1987; Sandler 1987). The Carnegie Commission's recent study on the undergraduate experience (Boyer 1986) reports that even today women are less likely to participate in class, and other studies support the conclusion (Krupnick 1985).

If women, who constitute a majority of students and mirror their male counterparts in social, economic, and academic background, encounter a chilly climate on campus, how might persons of different ethnic and racial backgrounds or older students or the disabled perceive the campus? In general, the theme that emerges from research, interviews, and general commentary is that many campuses are alienating for their students (Beckham 1988; Brown 1982; Burrell 1980; Elam 1982; Freedman 1981; McIntyre 1981; Mallinckrodt and Sedlacek 1987; Martin 1985; Oliver et al. 1985; Parker, Scott, and Chambers 1985; Ponterotto, Grieger, and Heaphy 1985; Rasor 1981; Suen 1983; Zuber 1981).

Minority students

Because of increasingly focused concern about minority enrollments and retention, a reasonably large body of literature discusses the campus environment experienced by minority students. Because of their numbers in the population and their longer history in higher education, the experience of African-American students provides the core of this literature (Allen 1982, 1986; Elam 1982; Loo and Rolison 1986; Morris 1979; Nettles 1986; Patterson and Sedlacek 1984; Peterson et al. 1978; Ponterotto, Grieger, and Heaphy 1985). The amount of literature is growing on Latinos, particularly Chicanos, however, and literature on the experience of Asian and Native American students is emerging (Chacon, Cohen, and Strover 1986; Hsia 1988; Madrozo-Peterson and Rodriguez 1978; Olivas 1986; Oliver et al. 1985; Patterson, Sedlacek, and Perry 1984; Rasor 1981; Sanders 1987; Sue 1981; Suen 1983; Webster 1984; White and Sedlacek 1987). A forthcoming publication will address the chilly climate for women of color.

While a large component of this literature focuses on the needs of minority students that result from lack of adequate preparation in specific areas, financial pressures, or lack of support and advising, another phenomenon, not often addressed as directly, emerges from the literature. Study after study reports the experiences of minority students from all backgrounds who encounter racism and overt or subtle forms of discrimination by other students or faculty. Many of these students experience culture shock by being in an environment where dominant values, expectations, or experiences may be very different from their own and may be implicitly or explicitly devalued (Allen 1982, 1986; Allen, Gurin, and Peterson 1988; Asamen and Berry 1987; Beckham 1988; Chew and Ogi 1987; Fiske 1988; Garza and Nelson 1973; Jaimes 1980; Oliver et al. 1985; Parker, Scott, and Chambers 1985; Sanders 1987; Sedlacek 1987; Sedlacek and Brooks 1976; Wright 1987; Zuber 1981). While poor academic preparation and socio-economic status may be a barrier to matriculation, evidence is growing that the poor quality of minority students' life on campus and their sense of isolation, alienation, and lack of support are more serious factors in attrition (Allen 1988b; Armstrong-West and de la Teja 1988; Bennett and Bean 1983; Crosson 1988; Jones, Harris, and Hand 1975). One important factor associated with success for African- American students is the degree of academic integration in campus life through the faculty and curriculum; on many campuses, integration is not sufficient in either academic or residential life (Nettles, Thoeny, and Gosman 1986). How is one to be integrated in this kind of environment?

Ask a black student about the racial climate on campus and he or she will likely describe it as a microcosm of society. . . . They hear outlandishly insensitive statements and observe painful expressions of disrespect and downright hatred. . . . Repeatedly, however, black experiences in mostly white colleges are chronicles of how the institutions have almost systematically bruised self-esteem and doled out mere pittances of support services (Beckham 1988, p. 76).

The issues surrounding the campus environment go deeper than individual acts of overt racism to more subtle questions concerning values and customs. Native American students, for whom soft speech and indirect eye contact are appropriate behaviors, suffer the consequences when confronted with an environment in which argument, assertiveness, and directness may not only be expected but also viewed as indicators of intellect and academic commitment (Sanders 1987). A comparison of perceptions of a university environment between Mexican-American and Anglo-American students found significant differences between their perceptions and comfort with such things as politeness, assertiveness, and risk taking (Garza and Nelson 1973). A number of studies on the learning styles of African-American, Native American, and Latino youth suggest more variety than is usually dealt with in traditional forms of pedagogy (Claxton and Murrell 1987). These patterns of difference reflect additional impediments to learning.

Research still suggests that white students have more negative attitudes toward African-Americans, particularly in intimate or personal interactions, while African-Americans are more likely to appreciate and value their interracial experiences (Carter, White, and Sedlacek 1985; Carver, Glass, and Katz 1978; Korolewicz and Korolewicz 1985; Le Flore 1982; Livingston and Stewart 1987; Martinez and Sedlacek 1983; Minatoya and Sedlacek 1984; Switkin and Gynther 1974). Ironically, despite common campus discussions about minority students who isolate themselves on campus, available research suggests that the amount of interracial contact among whites is much lower than it is for minorities (Dinka, Mazzella, and Pilant 1980). Given the relatively small number of minorities on many campuses, these results are not surprising, suggesting that we need to be cautious about how we define the problem. In this case, the problem may not be minority students who isolate themselves but nonminorities who avoid contact. The rising number of reports about racial incidents on campuses across the country document a problem that appears to be increasing, one that reflects growing tension in dealing with diversity (Bechman 1984; Rooks 1988; Weinberg 1982). A summary of the environment for racial and ethnic minorities on four-year campuses concludes that "while the scope and depth of racial and discriminatory attitudes and behavior are unknown, it is clear that many predominantly white four-year colleges and universities have somehow failed to live up to their ideals as civil and tolerant social communities that respect diversity and pluralism" (Crosson 1988, p. 381).

The adult learner

Attendance at a college or university for adult learners often requires the juggling of many roles. These students often attend part time, hold jobs off campus, and have significant family commitments. At the same time, they are often very persistent and have clear goals for their education. Some, such as women reentering college, have been out of school a long time, and others face significant financial pressures as they struggle to get an education. When the adult learner is also a woman of color, the number of barriers is multiplied (Pearson, Shavlik, and Touchton 1989). These factors provide challenges for both the student and the institution in terms of class schedules, child care, financial aid (which is often geared to the full-time student), career advisement, and access to the full range of services and programs. The student who cannot spend time on campus beyond the period spent in class cannot as easily learn about available services or how things are done or, indeed, experience the cultures of the campus itself. Many authors point out that the characteristics of the adult learner also have implications for methods of teaching and learning. Students expect that their academic program will not only acknowledge the validity of their own experiences but will also connect those experiences to their study. The literature suggests that the difference between the adult student and the traditional student presents significant challenges for teaching. The literature also describes the needs of adult students for emotional support and information (Bauer l981; Bodenkoop and Johansen 1980; Courage 1984; Creange 1980; Duhon 1986; Durnell 1980; Hetherington and Hudson 1981; Hu 1985; Knowles 1978; Saslow 1981; Soldler 1982).

Disabled students

The passage of Section 504 of the Rehabilitation Act of 1973 not only has facilitated and encouraged the enrollment of students with physical and learning disabilities but also validated the legitimacy of concerns about access for those with disabilities.

The needs of these students, particularly those with physical disabilities, raise fundamental questions about access and accessibility on campuses. Through architectural modifications, the restructuring of testing procedures and curricular requirements, and the availability of interpreters, tape recorders, computer systems, and support services for the learning disabled, more campus programs have been made available. In many cases, these modifications have made learning more beneficial and fruitful for students, faculty, and staff whose own learning or physical needs do not classify them as disabled but who nevertheless have special needs.

The need to reduce barriers for these students appears relatively straightforward, although from an institutional point of view, it requires commitment and expense. The literature suggests, however, that the need for physical or curricular enhancements is not the most formidable barrier those with disabilities face. Studies report the social isolation of disabled students that results from the discomfort experienced by the nondisabled in their interaction with them. Professor Seymour Martin Lipset, a well-known sociologist, author of more than 40 books, and himself dyslexic, described the isolation for such students as "punishing" (*Stanford Observer* 1989, p. 6). Social isolation is pertinent, not only because of the obvious emotional consequences for the individual but also because it creates a loss of access to critical, albeit informal, information on how to succeed. In dealing with the issue of social isolation, the emphasis seems to be on educating the disabled person rather than educating the institution or the majority culture to include those students who are different. Indeed, one line of research focuses on techniques that disabled students can use to increase the comfort level of nondisabled students. Yet surveys suggest a preponderance of negative attitudes faced by the disabled, evidence of avoidance behavior, and discomfort, suggesting that the disabled raise issues of vulnerability to others (Asch 1984; Belgrave 1984; Demetrulias, Sattler, and Graham 1982; Fenderson 1984; Patterson, Sedlacek, and Scales 1984; Richardson 1976; Stilwell, Stilwell, and Perril 1983; Yuker, Block, and Young 1966).

Summary
The kinds of experiences reflected in the literature suggest the diverse populations of students we have been dealing with:

- have a wide variety of needs for specific programs and services;
- have powerful and alienating experiences with racism,

discrimination, and stereotypic responses;
* have experienced campus attitudes and behaviors that isolate them;
* have experienced campuses that socially, physically, or programmatically (e.g., through the curriculum) communicate to them that they do not belong or are not welcome;
* have experienced a campus culture and value system that may not be consistent with their own background;
* feel the pressure to be exemplary, a phenomenon that is particularly strong for members of visible minorities whose numbers are small in the institution.

These experiences include needs and barriers that are quite specific in focus and scope, such as ramps and tutorial programs. Others result simply from being different or being a member of a visible minority. These experiences can stem from behaviors and incidents that reflect insensitivity to issues of difference, but they can also result from the experience of feeling that one does not belong. Such feelings can be based on visual and physical cues in the environment, by simple observation of who is in charge, or by how one is treated.

The significance of the quality of the environment is very important. It may both directly and indirectly affect performance and persistence. Experiences of alienation, lack of comfort, and isolation not only deprive students of access to information, support, and programs but can also produce stress and a general lack of commitment that the rigors of an education necessarily require (Allen 1988b; Etzioni 1968; Maynard 1980; Nettles 1988a; Olivas 1986; Rochin and de la Torres 1987; Seeman 1959; Uncapher et al. 1983; Zambrana 1987). "While isolation can be detrimental, cross-cultural contacts can be especially damaging if members of the majority bring with them significant measures of prejudice, intolerance, ignorance, or disdain" (SHEEO 1987, p. 33). If these issues are combined with deficits in academic preparation, the consequences of socioeconomic status, financial pressures, role conflicts, and family factors, it is not surprising that we see the negative figures related to retention and enrollment of groups different from the general population. These issues can be important for any member of the community who feels different but particularly for new students who at the same time are experiencing the transition to a new environment

(Hall 1984, 1986; Madden et al. 1987; SHEEO 1987; Williams and Siegmar 1978).

Deprivation has consequences for the rest of the community as well. The nontraditional student's lack of access to information and exchange results in lack of exchange for traditional students as well. It has long been argued that part of the reason students are required to learn other languages and about other cultures is that it broadens the student's understanding of society and how he or she is shaped by and in turn shapes the culture in which we live. The same reasoning applies to all aspects of diversity in an educational community (Bowser and Hunt 1981; Katz and Ivey 1977; Willie 1981).

THE ROLE OF STUDENT CHARACTERISTICS

In attempting to understand why some students succeed and others do not, research has focused on the role of background characteristics. Considerable caution must be exercised in interpreting the results of this approach. We are much clearer today that finding simple causal relationships is not possible. Moreover, by focusing attention on a narrow range of variables, we have restricted the investigation of other factors associated with success (Nettles 1988b).

The classic literature on persistence and college performance has generally concluded that background characteristics are some of the most reliable predictors of success. High school grade point average, socioeconomic status, Scholastic Aptitude Test (SAT) scores, and parental education have continually emerged to predict persistence or college Grade Point Average (GPA) (Astin 1975; Cope and Hannah 1975; Pantages and Creedon 1978). While most of that early literature did not differentiate among campus groups, except perhaps between men and women, the assumption remained that background characteristics were the most salient factors to look at to predict a student's success in college. Given that what is expected of a student in college is not unlike what is expected in high school, it is not unreasonable to pay serious attention to these factors. In coming to this conclusion, however, it is important to remember first that many of the early studies did not differentiate between voluntary and institutional dismissal. For some groups, academic background can play a more significant role in explaining academic failure. Second, while variables like high school GPA were often the largest predictors of persistence, they often accounted for only 10 to 12 percent of the variance in explaining persistence. In other words, academic background in many cases was not as potent an explanation of attrition as assumed (Tinto 1987). Moreover, the tendency was to describe such variables as SAT scores and high school GPA as measures of academic ability rather than academic preparation or background, suggesting that the problem is innate as opposed to a function of experience.

While recent research still focuses on traditional students and traditional measures of academic preparation, a growing body of research looks at other factors associated with the success of a variety of nontraditional populations. Much of this research is finding that not only do factors related to academic preparation continue to be important but that other

Educational deficits may not be nearly as important as the deficits that emerge from lack of self-confidence and from being in environments that question one's presence there.

factors are also important (Arciniega 1985; Astin 1982; Bean and Metzner 1985; Bennett and Okinaka 1984; Burrell 1980; Fields 1988; Lynch 1985; Nettles 1988b). *Leaving College,* a very significant book, summarizes the most current literature on persistence, including a careful look at what can be said about retention for a variety of different populations, and cites the importance of differentiating between those who leave voluntarily and those who are dismissed for academic reasons (Tinto 1987). It also points out the complex relationship between institutional characteristics and students' background characteristics as they relate to persistence. Using the National Longitudinal Study of the High School Class of 1972 as a base, Tinto points out that the differential in rates of persistence for African-Americans can be traced more to educational background than to class or race but that this statement is not true for Latino students for whom persistence is not related to academic preparation but may be related more to their collegiate experience. The presence of greater numbers of Latino students in two-year institutions, where retention is lower, likely plays a role in their attrition.

In addition to traditional background characteristics, the literature reflects the importance of such factors as the commitment to academic or occupational goals, the quality of the student's effort, good study habits, attitudinal characteristics, and other kinds of life experience as related to success (Astin 1975, 1985; DiCesare, Sedlacek, and Brooks 1972; Fields 1988; Nora 1987; Pace 1984; Wright et al. 1988). Important research has demonstrated the importance of noncognitive variables in predicting success (Sedlacek 1982; Tracey and Sedlacek 1984, 1985). This research comparing African-American and white students concludes that noncognitive factors like positive self-confidence, understanding of racism, realistic self-appraisal, and community involvement are more significant than academic ability in predicting persistence. Another study found dropout rates for whites related to academic variables but for African-Americans to a measure of social estrangement (Suen 1983). As mentioned earlier, preparation cannot explain the high dropout rates for Latinos (Tinto 1987). A very elegant study of Latinos in six community colleges found that commitment to the institution and to educational goals was an important indicator of retention (Nora 1987). And evidence suggests that for many students, particularly commuter students, older students, and Chicanas, external factors like family and work demands play significant roles in persistence and performance (Astin and Burciaga 1981; Bean and Metzner 1985; Chacon, Cohen, and Strover 1986; Zambrana 1987).

Throughout this literature, the role of gender is dealt with unevenly. Nevertheless, the complex interaction between such characteristics as race and gender cannot be overlooked. Chicanas experience a different kind of stress as a function of family and work demands (Zambrana 1987). An emerging theme in the literature concerns the declining presence of African-American males in higher education (Wilson 1988). Gender must be regarded as an important characteristic to be studied and understood along with race, culture, class, and disability (Bell-Scott 1984; Pearson, Shavlik, and Touchton 1989).

For all the years of research on the factors associated with persistence and performance, no clear answer exists to the question about the role of background characteristics. A danger is present, however, that the role of traditional measures of preparation continues to be overemphasized, thus overshadowing the role of the institution, the collegiate experience, and other noncognitive variables. For those already present in higher education, educational deficits may not be nearly as important as the deficits that emerge from lack of self-confidence and from being in environments that question one's presence there (Nettles 1988b). While traditional forms of academic preparation cannot be ignored, these elements play more of a role for some students than for others, for some forms of withdrawal than for others, and in some institutional contexts than in others. In terms of students' characteristics, other noncognitive factors need to be understood, considered, and emphasized. Moreover, the institutional responsibility for these issues cannot be ignored. The institution, the situation, and the student all play roles in students' success.

THE CHALLENGE OF INVOLVEMENT

Theories of Involvement

Many recent national reports about higher education as well as studies of enrollment management have echoed a similar theme: the importance of students' involvement in their own learning process. Tinto (1987) and Astin (1975, 1985) among others have developed major theoretical positions and spawned significant research that stress the importance of students' involvement in the academic enterprise. Both point out that the role of involvement can be both direct and indirect. Clearly, students are more apt to learn and to succeed if they are involved in their courses and involved with the curriculum. But research also shows that being involved with one's peers, with faculty outside the classroom, and with the institution can also facilitate success (Astin 1985; Fox 1985; Nettles and Johnson 1987; Pascarella 1980; Rooney 1985). Connections of this sort not only create a comfort level with the environment and offer academic and emotional support; they also provide access to information that facilitates adaptation to academic life beyond what is presented in handbooks and catalogs. Access to information has been cited as critically important to a number of nontraditional groups, particularly those who are part time and those who commute. Such students are especially vulnerable to the complications that come from "not knowing" (Creange 1980; Hetherington and Hudson 1981; Hu 1985; Nora 1987; Vaz 1987).

Tinto has developed a model of retention that has evolved from earlier models of student outcomes. His work is more explicit, however, in describing the complex interactions between background characteristics and the campus environment, positing that the fit between the student and the environment involves both social and academic integration in the institution. *Social integration* relates to involvement with peers, campus activities, and so on, while *academic integration* relates to academic performance, involvement with the curriculum, and contact with faculty and staff. Tinto suggests that when a student experiences integration, that student is more likely to persist. Importantly, lack of fit—or incongruence—occurs when the individual views himself or herself "at odds with the institution," a phrase that comes very close to describing the concept of alienation (Babbit, Bruback, and Thompson 1975; Braddock 1978; Loo and Rolison 1986).

A student's involvement—or lack of it—can be with different parts of the institution and can vary by degree. Clearly,

> *The challenge is to try to define values in which people can share but that at the same time allow for important differences to be acknowledged, even nourished.*

most institutions are comprised of any number of complex subcultures with which an individual might identify. Moreover, certain kinds of campuses, such as small institutions or residential campuses, may provide more opportunity for involvement than others. Based on his summary of the literature, Tinto suggests that centrality of the group is also an important factor; that is, the degree to which the group with which one identifies is perceived as being central to the institution is an important element fostering feelings of involvement with that institution. He cites some literature suggesting that the most effective support programs for minorities, for example, are those perceived to be central rather than peripheral to the institution. The implications are important. In particular, it might not be sufficient for an individual student to be involved with just any group if he or she perceives that that group is marginal to the institution.

A reasonable amount of research now supports Tinto's model. Some of the work investigating the different forms of integration—academic or social, informal or formal—suggests that one or the other might be more important for different groups under different circumstances. Not surprisingly, the results are not entirely consistent, suggesting that many factors are related to the significance of involvement. One study found that dropout behavior for African-American students was related to social estrangement (Suen 1983), and a study of African-American and white men and women found that social integration is more important for African-American men, that both academic and social integration are significant for African-American women, and that academic integration is most important for whites (Stoecker, Pascarella, and Wolfe 1988).

These factors of race and gender may also interact with the type of institution. For African-American students at historically African-American colleges, academic integration appears to relate to success, whereas some have found that social integration is more important at traditionally white institutions for African-American males (Pascarella 1985). Other research suggests, however, that the danger of too much social integration and not enough academic integration can be a negative factor for African-American men at white institutions (Nettles, Thoeny, and Gosman 1987). Others have found that black colleges tend to achieve greater academic integration for both African-American and white students, including greater involvement on the part of African-American and white faculty in the lives of students (Allen 1987; Fleming 1984; Gurin and Epps 1975; Nettles, Thoeny, and Gosman 1987). A study of Latinos in six community colleges found that educational goals and institutional commitment were mediated by factors of involvement (Nora 1987).

Astin has also emphasized the importance of involvement to academic success. By building on research related to learning theory, earlier studies involving the quality of effort (Pace 1984), and his own work, Astin concludes that involvement in learning and involvement in campus life are critical factors in institutions' and students' success. By involvement, he means the "amount of physical and psychological energy that the student devotes to the academic experience" (Astin 1985, p. 36). The implication is that the effectiveness of any program can be assessed by the quality and degree of students' involvement.

Astin suggests, however, that the goal of involvement is often difficult to accomplish, because some fundamental values within academic life run counter to it. The lack of progress in improving learning can partly be ascribed to a basic conflict between deep values rooted in the academic tradition and the conditions that tend to promote success and learning. It is now understood that learning and the commitment to learning are best accomplished in an environment of cooperation and support and that such an environment is most likely to promote involvement. Competition, which has been so important to many campuses, is increasingly being recognized as detrimental for many students (Astin 1987; Belenky et al. 1986; Martin 1985; Palmer 1987; Sanders 1987; Sandler 1987; Sandler and Hall 1982). Grading on a curve, for example, is problematic because it puts people in comparison with one another, with the success of a few serving to impede the success of others. Universal success is impossible when using such a curve. This structure reinforces a competitive environment that is facilitated by the need and desire of today's students to succeed (Astin 1987). Indeed, faculty who create alternative structures in which all students can succeed have been accused of contributing to grade inflation and have frequently been soundly criticized for their approaches.

The research to date has been unusually successful in supporting the importance of integration and involvement as important factors in persistence and success. While much work needs to be done in understanding the nature and importance of involvement for nontraditional groups, the research here also suggests the significance of the concept. In light of it, earlier descriptions of noninvolvement and alienation become particularly significant. We find evidence of noninvolvement—indeed alienation—on campuses for many nontraditional students. Such findings may help explain why so many students do not perform up to their potential.

The sources of the alienation may originate from a variety of experiences, ranging from racial discrimination to a sense of "not belonging." Some of the alienation may also be attributed to the presence of certain values in the institution that conflict with an individual's own patterns of learning or culture. Competition, which can be antithetical to learning for anyone, may be particularly difficult for groups whose own cultures emphasize cooperation. If the challenge of diversity is to be met, campuses must confront these issues.

> *Being the other is feeling different, is awareness of being distinct, is consciousness of being dissimilar. It means being outside the game, outside the circle, outside the set. . . . Otherness results in feeling excluded, closed out, precluded, even disdained and scorned. It produces a sense of isolation, of apartness, of disconnectedness, of alienation* (Madrid 1988, p. 2).

In contemporary higher education, the condition of diversity is all too often a condition of alienation. If the theories and research on the central importance of involvement are true, these conditions must change. Several bodies of literature outside higher education add perspective to understanding the complexity of the challenge of involving students of diverse backgrounds in our institutions. The literatures on cultural pluralism, intergroup relations, and demography suggest important elements to be considered.

Cultural Pluralism

If institutions are to meet the challenge of diversity and create campuses in which students are truly involved, it is clear that how we conceive of the institution needs to be clarified. Despite the discussions about increasing diversity in the student body, the underlying assumption in much of the literature has appeared to be that the goal for students is assimilation into the dominant values and characteristics of the university (Blackwell 1987; Hunt 1975). Indeed, some observers believe that the groups most successful in integrating into American society and education have been those whose own backgrounds were closest to the dominant European traditions in the culture or those who gave up their identities to be "Americanized" (Castaneda 1974; Gordon 1964; Peterson et al. 1978; Rokeach 1972; Sue 1981). Whether assimilation is an appropriate goal and if so to what norm one should assimilate are important questions at the forefront of the issue of diversity today. For women, "assimilation has been viewed as the path to equality . . . [but] assimilation at the expense of femaleness becomes not only undesirable but a kind of death" (Desjardins 1989, p. 144). Many who struggle with what it means to be different have echoed such a view.

In contrast to the notion of assimilation, the term "cultural pluralism" has emerged to signify a society and community in which diversity is valued and in which difference can coexist with the concept of community (Astin 1984; McBay 1986; Terry 1981).

The literature includes many different metaphors and models for cultural pluralism and reflects some underlying contradictions in our understanding of pluralism and our language for it (Banks 1981; Quevedo-Garcia 1987). Moreover, the view of what a culturally pluralistic society looks like varies. The cultural separatist provides for the maintenance of separate cultures that coexist as long as one group does not infringe on the rights of another, and the emphasis is on cultural preservation. The cultural diffusion model suggests that interaction among groups, interethnic social relationships, and the borrowing of traditions will occur. Some who propose this model as the ideal also maintain that because the Anglo-American tradition is dominant in this culture, everyone must acquire certain of the traits associated with it to succeed. This view suggests a bicultural model in which the dominant culture does not change but the individuals become facile in moving between their personal culture and the culture of the society. A third model describes cultural fusion in which diverse cultures come together to form a new culture that reflects and integrates the best of many cultures (Watson 1980).

A pluralistic approach acknowledges and stresses ethnic or group identity (Hunt 1975). A recent report on the racial climate at MIT defines pluralism as "a social condition . . .

in which several distinct ethnic, religious, and racial communities live side by side, willing to affirm each other's dignity, ready to benefit from each other's experiences, and quick to acknowledge each other's contributions to the common welfare" (McBay 1986, p. 2). A thoughtful analysis of the concept of cultural pluralism suggests that several problems are involved with proposing the model of cultural pluralism without addressing some of its limits (Suzuki 1984). As defined by MIT, for example, cultural pluralism adopts a kind of federalist approach to diversity that focuses on the distinctiveness of each group without acknowledging any unifying values or goals. This idealized model, however, suggests that by allowing for group identity, issues of racism, sexism, classism, or homophobia will disappear, an assumption that is not likely to be valid. It also does not reflect the need to deal with the conflict that will inevitably result. The needs of the group may conflict with those of the larger community or other groups, and such conflicts must be resolved. One of Suzuki's most challenging reflections is that the existing social structure, particularly large centralized bureaucracies, may make the achievement of true cultural pluralism impossible. The idea of communities living "side by side" reflects some degree of autonomy and self-control in matters that our large public bureaucracies make very difficult (Suzuki 1984).

A creative tension clearly exists between the call for involvement and the call for pluralism. Involvement in the institution suggests the ability to share certain values or goals, while pluralism leaves open the possibility of living parallel but separate lives. It would appear that the challenge is to try to define values in which people can share but that at the same time allow for important differences to be acknowledged, even nourished. Rather than similarity, diversity, whether in technology, geography, religion, or origins, is the natural order of things, and the founding values of this country were based on shared values about diversity, requiring the resolution of issues of community versus individual rights (Madrid 1988). This tension is certainly apparent in the U.S. Constitution with respect to matters of state and federal jurisdiction. It also appears in higher education literature, where a creative tension exists between those who argue for the importance of academic freedom and creative anarchy and those who argue for the importance of shared values and organizational culture (Clark 1972; Masland 1985; Weick 1976).

Resolving these tensions requires reflectiveness about institutional goals and values and about the ways in which "shared values" on the one hand and the "value of diversity" on the other can be brought together. Such an effort is complicated by the impact that power differentials, inequality, and past experiences have on institutional discussions. And being in a minority or majority position changes the way one approaches these questions (Wilkerson 1989).

It also requires an acknowledgment that conflicts will emerge and that institutions that are prepared for the challenge of diversity will also be prepared for conflict and thus will have the means for resolving conflicts. If the challenge of a pluralistic institution is to create a process where each student will experience an environment that accepts his or her preferred modes of relating, communicating, and learning as equally important (Castaneda 1974), then the challenges to higher education cannot be underestimated, particularly in large bureaucratic structures where multiple choice tests, large lecture halls, and little interaction may be the prevailing modes. Such a model also presupposes knowledge and respect and a desire to learn among each of these groups and the institution.

Intergroup Relations

A long tradition of research and scholarship has grown out of concern for furthering interracial cooperation in this country. The dominant questions have centered on the characteristics that would promote harmony among groups (Allport 1954; Pettigrew 1985). In light of the challenges of diversity, this literature contributes significant perspectives. "Intergroup relations represent in their enormous scope one of the most difficult and complex knots of problems [that] we confront in our time" (Tajfel 1982, p. 1). The early assumptions had been that simply promoting contact among people would improve relationships. The now-classic *Nature of Prejudice* points out that simple proximity among people of different backgrounds is not enough and began to try to specify conditions under which such interactions would be positive (Allport 1954). It concludes that these interactions would be successful only if those involved *possess equal status, seek common goals, depend cooperatively on one another, and interact with the positive support of authorities, laws, and customs.* Nevertheless, achieving cooperation among groups is difficult because a pattern of favoritism develops among members of the same group. Any tendencies to categorize people naturally leads to an in-group, out-group division in which members of one's own group are inclined to be favored, particularly in a context of conflict or when the status of different groups differs (Konrad and Gutek 1987). As a result, simple proximity of individuals will not produce the kind of involvement and interaction one would hope for. It also appears that it is difficult to stop people from making categorical divisions. Simply placing people into groups tends to enhance the view that they are significantly different. In the case of visible minorities, women, the physically disabled, or older students, it may not be possible to avoid such categorizations. Thus, those who argue that institutions should not focus on the diversity within the campus may be ignoring the reality that such divisions will occur.

Certain conditions may *increase* intergroup tension and prejudice:

1. When the contact produces competition;
2. When the contact is unpleasant and involuntary;
3. When the prestige or status of one group is lowered as a result of contact;
4. When members of a group or the group as a whole are in a state of frustration;
5. When the groups have moral or ethical standards objectionable to the other;
6. When the minority is of lower status or lower in any relevant characteristic (Amir 1969, pp. 338–39).

The conditions for conflict rather than cooperation among groups are clearly present on many campuses (Epps 1974). Nevertheless, this literature has also begun to point out to organizations the benefits of facing these challenges rather than viewing them as a complication. A recent review of the literature suggests that the negative impact of this pattern of discrimination between groups can be reduced by stressing cooperation among groups, by encouraging contact between groups based on true equality, and by facilitating membership in several groups (Tajfel 1982). This last item has important significance in this area. Theoretically, individuals who hold memberships in several groups begin to break down the rigid notions of "in" group and "out" group that form the basis of tensions and stereotyping among groups. By participating in both, they facilitate the reduction of stereotyping within either group. The support of policies, procedures, and customs is also critical (Asch 1984; Tajfel 1982).

One conclusion to be drawn from this literature is that simple proximity is not enough. Proximity creates potential, but it does not necessarily promote the kinds of goals for involvement that are central to a quality education (Johnson, Johnson, and Mariyama 1983). Moreover, when individuals of differing status come together without appropriate support and without mutually beneficial tasks, the climate may be negative.

Institutions addressing the challenge of diversity need to address issues of status groupings, institutional support and climate, membership in several groups, and significant contact in which the task is functionally important. The nature of many of today's institutions, combined with increasing enrollments of students of many different kinds of backgrounds, may explain some of the tension occurring today on college campuses.

Demography

While the phrase "changing demographics" found today in the literature of higher education is taken to mean changing numbers of different populations of students, the study of demographics can provide important perspectives on how organizations will function. The demography of an organization refers to its composition in terms of basic attributes like age, sex, educational level, and length of employment. At its most basic, organizational demographics focuses on the significance of numbers. It is argued that the composition of an organization broadly affects institutional characteristics like interpersonal and intergroup interaction, morale, turnover, and performance. Kanter (1977) describes in great detail the ways in which proportional representation of groups can affect how people in an organization relate to one another, in particular focusing on the significance of being the only one, or the token member, of any visible minority. In many ways, what she describes is a no-win situation in which members of the minority or the majority will not find a comfortable way of relating.

When a group achieves 20 percent of a population, issues of tokenism appear to decrease. Groups of individuals who hold smaller proportions are vulnerable to increased visibility,

scrutiny, and pressure, which can result in reduced performance and increased psychological stress (Kanter 1977; Mingle 1987; Pfeffer 1983, 1985). Extreme tokenism, being the
only one of a group, may also promote a conservatism that
does not at all reflect diversity; that is, the individual is under
pressure to look and act like the majority if she or he is to
succeed. Of course, it is done at a significant cost to the person's own integrity and sense of effectiveness (Martin 1985;
Sandler 1987).

A set of apparently contradictory consequences occur when
one describes the condition of being in the minority, and
these conditions seem to exist simultaneously. The first is that
being in such a position has benefits and disadvantages (Konrad and Gutek 1987; Phillips and Blumberg 1982). A visible
minority invariably becomes the focus of attention and as such
might benefit from being noticed. At the same time, being
the focus of attention means one comes under greater scrutiny
and stress. Being "'the other' is invisible" while at the same
time "sticking out like a sore thumb" (Madrid 1988).

The impact of different proportions also is somewhat contradictory. Theoretically, as the numbers of minorities
increase, more opportunities should exist for contact and the
breaking down of stereotypes. But some evidence indicates
that as numbers increase, the majority group becomes more
threatened, particularly when persons of differential status
are involved. It may be that as numbers increase, it is more
comfortable for minorities but less comfortable, at least for
a period, for the majority (Kanter 1977; Konrad and Gutek
1987; Kraiger and Ford 1985; Loo and Rolison 1986).

The literature on campus environments provides some support for these propositions and their apparent contradictions.
With the exception of women and adult learners, most groups
under discussion here constitute a minority at the present
time. All ethnic minorities combined still constitute less than
20 percent of the enrollment in higher education. The issue
of tokenism therefore remains central even when individual
minority groups are blended together. When these groups
are viewed separately, issues of tokenism become even more
evident.

Summary
While it is challenging to draw conclusions from such a wide-
ranging array of theory and research as presented in the liter-

atures on involvement, demography, pluralism, and intergroup relations, we can conclude that:

1. Involvement and integration—formal or informal, academic or social—are critical elements for success. The literatures on academic integration and intergroup relations support the importance of involvement.

2. While an institution can assume that creating formal and informal opportunities for involvement is important, we need to pay careful attention to whether the forms of that involvement will be different for different groups and individuals. African-Americans and Chicanos may experience such efforts differently from international students or recent immigrant groups. Furthermore, it must be recognized that variations across different kinds of institutions will exist as well. What can or will work at one place may not work at another.

3. Highly competitive environments may be detrimental not only to learning but also to creating opportunities for collaboration and memberships in several groups so important for pluralistic communities.

4. Centrality is a key dimension as one evaluates participation and programs. Involvement is more significant when it is closer to the center of rather than peripheral to the institution's mission. Institutions must pay attention to the ways in which students are encouraged to become involved and the ways in which those students *perceive* the forms of involvement. The higher education community has talked about the importance of diversity for some years, but without visible and tangible signs of that centrality, others may not perceive the message.

5. Having significant enough numbers in a group helps provide the variety and "critical mass" to reduce the consequences of tokenism. A figure of 20 percent is often mentioned as a critical point. But having sufficient numbers and proportions is not enough. Without sufficient numbers, efforts at creating communities that are comfortable with diversity will be difficult. Having sufficient numbers does not guarantee a successful educational experience.

6. Being a member of a nontraditional population is all too often synonymous with alienation. If involvement and integration are essential ingredients for success, this con-

nection must be broken.

7. The literature on intergroup relations suggests that simple contact among diverse groups will not in itself create an environment that values diversity. Factors such as unequal status, perceived lack of institutional support, a competitive climate, and lack of significant common tasks can lead to conflict and frustration.

8. Students will do better in environments that are open, accepting, and affirming. Efforts to establish cooperation and trust are critical to creating environments in which students can be involved. Such efforts, however, raise questions of institutional, group, and individual values that may need to be addressed if a connection between the institution and its students is to be firmly established. Creating environments that are open in these ways will sometimes confront the behaviors and attitudes of the majority.

9. Institutions will need to discuss the meaning of pluralism, those values for which the institution stands, and those values around which differences can exist.

10. Institutions will need to know much more about students, groups, and institutional processes. Demographic information on the institution, perceptions about the environment, data on the group affiliations of students, and the degree of interaction among students and student groups can be essential.

11. Institutions need to be sensitive to the difficult role of those in token positions (whether intentional or not) and to some of the inevitable strains it will create.

12. Conflict will be an inevitable part of the process of creating educational communities in a pluralistic context. In addition, some of the conditions for intergroup tension (unequal status, lack of shared tasks, and so on) are present on many campuses today.

The research on involvement and intergroup relations calls for greater opportunities for cooperative tasks. The literatures on cultural pluralism and demography point out the ways in which creating such opportunities will be difficult. The challenge of diversity rests on meeting the objectives of involvement along with and perhaps through pluralism. The classic work, *The Impact of College on Students,* describes the kind of colleges and universities with the greatest potential for educational impact as those with a clear sense of mission and students from diverse backgrounds (Feldman and Newcomb 1969). Such institutions may be the most successful in creating involvement through the kind of commitment to shared purposes that Allport describes. At the same time, the diversity of backgrounds contributes varieties of perspectives to the questions at hand. Institutions with numbers of diverse populations but no sense of shared purposes may invite attrition because no one feels involved in the institution. Overly homogeneous institutions may have a difficult time facilitating learning. In this context, diversity can be viewed as an essential element to the creation of a truly educational community.

INSTITUTIONAL RESPONSES TO DIVERSITY

Approaches of Successful Institutions

Some striking similarities occur in the conclusions of many studies that have looked at "successful" institutions, even when a variety of student populations are being considered. Many focus on the need to develop strong programmatic responses that attempt to facilitate academic and social integration and are therefore quite consistent with the theories of involvement. In general, these institutions concentrate on five areas:

Specific programmatic and policy responses by themselves are not sufficient to make major strides . . . more fundamental organizational shifts are required.

1. *Providing students with the tools to succeed.* At successful institutions, student assistance is viewed as comprehensive and central to the institution, and the quality of instruction is a high priority. Students are therefore free to take advantage of all resources without stigma. In addition to academic support services, financial assistance, tutoring, and technical support, such programs also focus on intensive advising programs that use faculty and students as mentors and follow up through the monitoring and evaluation of students' progress (Blake 1987; Cardoza 1986; Gittell 1985; Glennen, Boxley, and Farren 1985; Richardson and de los Santos 1988; Valencia Community College 1981).

2. *Developing increased coordination with the sector involving kindergarten through grade 12 and articulation between sectors.* Early academic preparation and the development of long-term educational goals are important factors in matriculation. As a result, successful institutions have begun to develop programs with elementary and secondary schools to assist in the process of identifying students who aspire to college, helping students set goals, educating counselors, and working with teachers (Blakely 1987; Nelms 1982; Richardson and de los Santos 1988; SHEEO 1987). In addition, such institutions recognize that many nontraditional students begin their college careers in community colleges. Articulation programs, counseling, data collection, appropriate curricula, and financial assistance are all important features of efforts to facilitate and encourage the transition among sectors of higher education (Mingle 1987; Richardson and Bender 1987).

3. *Creating an "accepting" campus climate or an "academic environment that nourishes and encourages students to succeed"* (Commission on Minority Participation 1988; Rendon and Nora 1988; Shavlik, Touchton, and Pearson

1989). These efforts invariably move beyond a focus directed simply toward students and their needs to acknowledging the role of institutional policies, procedures, and programs in affecting the creation of a positive climate for diversity. These efforts inevitably include all members of the campus community, and central to them are the diversification of the curriculum, faculty, and staff, the addition of policies and procedures that attempt to ensure that appropriate values and standards of expected behavior are clear and diligently enforced, and the creation of personal and programmatic support systems that encourage involvement and success at all levels.

4. *Developing access to adequate information and a good data base that focuses on students, the barriers they face, and the factors associated with successful completion of their programs.* Because of the obvious diversity in the needs of different students and the diversity in campus structures and mission, each institution monitors itself and its students.

5. *Providing strong and focused leadership.* The importance of campus leadership is often mentioned as critical to whatever institutional efforts are made. Effective leadership from the faculty and administration helps to create an institutional agenda and to convey the significance of the efforts. Strong institutional statements may also help alleviate some of the risk often taken by those who are in the minority when they speak out on institutional and curricular matters (Carodo and Mangano 1982; Clewell and Ficklen 1986; Gittell 1985; Goldberg et al. 1985; Hu 1985; Lang 1987; Larwood, Gutek, and Gattiker 1984; Neher 1985; Parker, Scott, and Chambers 1985; Peterson et al. 1978; Roueche and Baker 1987; Shavlik, Touchton, and Pearson 1989; Soldier 1982; Spaights, Dixon, and Nicholas 1985).

Lessons from the women's colleges

No single sector of higher education has been able to respond fully to all aspects of the diversity that is discussed here. Lessons can be learned, however, from institutions whose missions are dedicated to one or the other groups under consideration. These environments make explicit the support for their constituency, providing a de facto statement of the priority given this goal in all that the institution does. Whether the institution is a Gallaudet University dedicated to deaf stu-

dents, a historically African-American college, a college dedicated to Native Americans, or a women's college, these institutions are important. To the degree that they are special, they
can be models for other institutions of what is needed if one
is to create institutions truly dedicated to educating the diversity of students today. The literatures on women's colleges
and historically African-American institutions were reviewed
for this purpose. These literatures also point to the barriers
that these institutions face in their goals to educate particular
populations.

Observers generally agree that women's colleges, even
while controlling for selectivity, have in the past graduated
and continue to graduate a greater percentage of women
achievers than comparable coeducational colleges (Oates and
Williamson 1978; Rice and Hemmings 1988; Tidball 1988).
Many of the writers involved engage in discussion and debate
about the factors associated with this success and in particular
whether it is a function of the institution or the kind of student who attends. Some have attributed it less to the environment and programs of these colleges than to the kinds
of students who have attended (Oates and Williamson 1978).
Indeed, it is difficult to sort out all these relationships and
to establish clear cause-and-effect relationships among such
things as selectivity, environment, and success. Nevertheless,
agreement is general about what graduates of women's colleges have achieved, the level of students' satisfaction, and
the kind of climate created (Rice and Hemmings 1988).

Women's colleges—those that are historically African-
American and those that are predominantly white—have been
able to provide an environment in which women are seen
as central and in which women are present in diverse roles
throughout the faculty and staff. Only in women's colleges
does anything close to equity exist in terms of faculty status,
membership, and rank, and it is from the women's colleges
that the vast majority of women college presidents come
("The College President" 1988; Simmons 1978; Women's College Coalition 1981).

Some have demonstrated a remarkably high correlation
between the proportion of women on the faculty and the rate
of women achievers in those institutions, leading to the conclusion that the presence of women on the faculty is one of
the most important factors in women's achievement (Tidball
1973, 1976, 1980). Even those who believe that not enough

consideration is given to students' entering characteristics have concurred with the importance of this factor and an environment that speaks to women's specialness and capacity for success (Oates and Williamson 1978).

Women's colleges have not always been leaders in curricular innovation out of fear of having their curricula negatively compared to traditional institutions. Even so, their curricula and teaching have been more apt to reflect women's concerns, simply because they were more likely to be taught by and to women (Stimpson 1987). Moreover, evidence suggests that male faculty at women's colleges also explicitly support the goals of women's education (Women's College Coalition 1981). In addition, the environment of women's colleges challenges women to become all those things they are not asked to be in many "coeducational" environments. They are faculty and student leaders, chairs of committees, merit award recipients, mentors, and beneficiaries of mentors. The environment of these colleges provides opportunities for varieties of leadership styles, for success and failure, and for nonstereotypic approaches to women and "their" issues. Research conducted even in recent years points out that women behave differently and are treated differently when they are in all-female environments than when they are in coed groups or when they are taught by women rather than by men (Krupnick 1985).

Because of the same attitudes that often confront women concerning their value or importance, women's colleges have to deal with society's perceptions and often feel they have to take a conservative approach with respect to women's education to prove their value. Many also have been on the defensive about their successes. The result has been that fewer of these institutions are left to provide models of what institutions dedicated to women can mean.

Lessons from the historically African-American institutions

While one can debate the role of selectivity in explaining the rates of achievement for graduates of women's colleges, this issue is not as much of a factor in discussing the achievement of the historically African-American colleges, particularly in recent years. Known for educating students with wide-ranging academic backgrounds, these institutions are further challenged by fewer resources than other institutions and increasing competition for their students. Nevertheless, these institutions account for a much greater share of African-American degrees at all levels than their enrollments would account for and have demonstrated success for a broader range of students than have traditionally white institutions (Cross and Astin 1981; Fleming 1984; Green 1989; Gurin and Epps 1975; Hart 1984; McClain 1979; Maryland State Board 1981; Smith 1981; Wilson 1988).

One analysis of the rate of degrees completed suggests clearly that traditionally African-American institutions, along with some selective northeastern universities, have had the most success in terms of graduation rates (Hart 1984). The ACE's recent handbook supports this analysis, noting that in 1984–85 they awarded 34 percent of the BA degrees while enrolling only 18 percent of African-American students (Green 1989). In addition, 50 percent of the African-American faculty in white research universities received their undergraduate degrees at historically African-American colleges and universities (Wilson 1988).

The literature contains considerable disagreement about other benefits of attending either white or African-American institutions. These studies rely heavily on statistical data, but the approaches and the sources of data yield different conclusions. Researchers, many employing multivariate statistical techniques, have looked at whether institutional type makes a significant difference when such factors as background characteristics are controlled. The results are mixed. A study of African-American students at both white and African-American institutions found greater cognitive development and higher aspirations among African-American students attending African-American institutions (Fleming 1984). It also noted that African-American women become more assertive at white institutions. Another researcher has not found institutional type in general to be a predictor of success (Pascarella 1985). Some have found mixed benefits from attending traditionally African-American or white institutions in terms of speed of completion and performance (Nettles 1988a). For example, one study found that African-American students are more likely to complete the degree in four years at a traditionally African-American institution but may have some career advantages if they attend a traditionally white institution, presumably because of the access to "the mainstream" (Braddock and McPartland 1988). The conclusions from this kind of research go to the heart of concerns about society, because they suggest that success in a career may be related to having access to people in power and that such access may be more readily available in traditionally white institutions.

The evidence suggests that the impact of attending one kind of institution over the other varies with the particular nature of the institution and its resources, the particular student involved, and other factors, such as gender (Allen 1988b; Fleming 1984; Pascarella, Smart, and Stoecker 1989). Numbers of authors point to the sometimes difficult choices that students are asked to make between access to prestige and resources against access to personal growth and satisfaction (Allen 1988b). They generally agree, however, that historically African-American colleges and universities succeed in involving students academically as well as providing environments that make their success a central part of the institution's mission. These institutions accommodate both educational equity and intellectual development in a common mission. Authors point to the generally positive climate in these institutions, taking the form of wider networks of friendship, more opportunities for involvement, and greater expectations for success (Allen 1988b; Fleming 1984; Gillespie 1983; Gurin and Epps 1975; Morris 1979; Nettles 1986; SHEEO 1987). Historically African-American colleges have served and continue to serve an important role in higher education by providing the bulk of African-American leadership and advanced degrees through an environment that offers tools for success, a sense of centrality, and sufficient numbers to eliminate issues of tokenism for African-American students and faculty. Furthermore, their admissions standards "are as sensitive to the *potential* of black applicants as they are to the limits of their precollege backgrounds" (Morris 1979, p. 201).

Summary

What are the lessons learned from the colleges dedicated to serving a particular group? As with the characteristics of successful institutions listed earlier, these institutions focus on the success of their students and presume their capacity for success. This effort is clearly facilitated by the presence of many faculty and administrators who provide role models and varieties of perspectives. Sufficient numbers enhance success and the opportunity for variety, something that is more difficult to achieve when the community contains few minorities, women, or disabled. These institutions also tend to provide whatever programmatic support is necessary as part of the educational program. All in all, a special environment—in many ways a more benign environment—exists in which individuals learn without their race or gender functioning as a stigma in their performance.

Implications: An Expanded Focus

What women's colleges can assume for women, other colleges and universities cannot assume for their students. What traditionally African-American institutions can assume for African-American students, others cannot assume. Yet most students do not attend these kinds of institutions, and challenges and benefits are inherent in whatever choice is made. The last 20 years have provided a myriad of opportunities for institutions to look at the issues related to diversity and to respond to them. The characteristics of successful institutions, women's colleges, and historically African-American colleges and universities include programs and support services that focus on the particular needs of particular students and groups while also creating organizational climates that are positive and supportive of students' diversity. A number of handbooks and program descriptions available in the literature describe some of the successful institutional approaches to meeting a variety of students' needs (Clewell and Ficklen 1986; Richardson, Simmons, and de los Santos 1987; WICHE 1987). While some, such as ACE's *Minorities on Campus* (Green 1989), address programs for minority students and others, such as *Educating the Majority* (Pearson, Shavlik, and Touchton 1989), address women's concerns, the themes are sufficiently consistent to be of critical importance for all institutions. The dominant focus in many of these approaches is still on the needs of the particular student group and appropriate institutional responses to those needs. This monograph began by noting how important the phrasing of questions is in shaping the answers that follow. Here again this issue must be addressed. The basic conceptual framework for many of the more traditional responses to diversity has focused on *student assistance.* Tutorial services, financial aid, ramps and braille maps, and academic support programs all reflect an effort to respond to problems that students bring with them. Fundamentally, it is a "deficit" approach to diversity in that it attempts to improve success by providing the student with support and resources. In many institutions, response has been broadened considerably through efforts to address the climate of the institution for these students. Campuses have added ethnic studies programs, ethnic support centers, women's studies programs, evening classes, and other institutional changes. These efforts to provide *institutional accommodation* still focus on the "special needs" of nontraditional students but acknowledge ways in which the institution can present barriers to success.

More and more, however, what appears throughout the literatures on the many groups that have been relegated to the margin is a set of themes requiring a shift in the ways we approach the challenge of diversity and the focus of the issue. By asking *how* an institution begins to educate and create a climate that is involving for all its members, the question is focused on fundamental aspects of the institution and its ability to embrace diversity, rather than on its ability to simply add programs or make modest changes. Recognition is increasing that specific programmatic and policy responses by themselves are not sufficient to make major strides and that more fundamental organizational shifts are required. Without this shift, all other approaches (while still important and essential) run the risk of simply helping students "adjust," "manage," or "survive" in an alien environment. "Unfortunately, many critics have been so impressed by the newly erected monuments to equal opportunity that they have failed to recognize that the foundations are the same as those [that] have for centuries perpetuated a structure of inequality of opportunity" (Morris 1979, p. 273). A similar theme is voiced on the education of women: "Now is the time for our institutions of higher education to reshape organizational structures, question institutional values, reexamine policies and procedures, and develop plans to sincerely meet the needs of women, faculty, administrators, staff, and students" (Pearson, Shavlik, and Touchton 1989, p. 8). The need is present to build on and maintain the efforts of those successful institutions that focus on individuals' and groups' needs and at the same time to focus on all students, all faculty, and the institution's capacity to *organize for diversity.*

ORGANIZING FOR DIVERSITY: Fundamental Issues

Higher education is faced today with the necessity—and the opportunity—to once again rethink what it does and how it does it. At the core of this effort is the organization's improved capacity to educate in a pluralistic society for a pluralistic world. But to do so requires a shift in our thinking from a focus on the issues surrounding students and "the problems" they create for the institution. In addition to whether students are prepared for learning is a serious question as to whether institutions are prepared for diversity. Such a shift requires a different rationale for thinking about change. If the institution is concerned about the capacity to deal with diversity, then the attention is on the entire community. Diversity among faculty, staff, and students is seen as important not only for the support such individuals provide for specific groups but also for the importance of diverse perspectives to institutional success and quality. The institution recognizes that remediation is an issue for many students and that concern for effective teaching and learning must be a paramount objective throughout the institution. Readiness to deal with diversity requires asking about the attitudes and information of traditional students as well as nontraditional students. Indeed, at a number of institutions, programs have been developed that focus on multicultural awareness for all students through workshops and course credit. Such programs assume that individuals need education about and awareness of pluralism. The message is that educating for diversity is important for everyone to create a suitable environment for diversity, both in the university and in society (Banks 1981; Barbarin 1981).

On many campuses across the country, the challenges of creating an organization that embraces diversity so that it can truly begin to educate all students has begun.

Institutional self-reflection, let alone transformation, is not an easy process. It raises questions about the institution and its assumptions about the academic enterprise. Moreover, the picture of what colleges and universities should look like is not yet clear, though the research on successful institutions suggests some of the issues that institutions must address. Higher education is a highly complex, decentralized system, and within that system is an enormous array of institutions. Thus, the process of change and the specific goals for change will necessarily be specific to the institution. Nevertheless, the existing review of the literature suggests that colleges and universities—large and small, commuter and residential, pub-

In addition to whether students are prepared for learning is a serious question as to whether institutions are prepared for diversity.

lic and private, urban and rural—will be asked to confront
a number of challenges as diversity is addressed.

Diversification of Faculty and Staff

The call for a more diversified faculty and staff in the literature
is viewed almost universally as important. The literature is
clear about the importance of faculty support in general and
the importance of this role in particular for nontraditional students, whether adult learners, disabled students, or minority
students. Certainly an important aspect of the success of historically African-American colleges and women's colleges rests
on the important role of African-American faculty and staff
and women faculty and staff in running the institution. The
emphasis on a diverse faculty and staff is indeed critical but
for more reasons than are often articulated.

Five reasons emerge. The first three deal with faculty and
staff roles relating to students. The most common reason
given for the need to diversify faculty and staff is to provide
support for the benefit of students from particular groups.
Observers generally acknowledge that students in the minority
will seek out a faculty member who, they perceive, understands their experience. Often this selection is based on gender, racial or ethnic commonality, or disability. Given the environment on many campuses, such faculty and staff play a very
important role. Indeed, evidence suggests that such faculty
and staff, because of their relatively small numbers, are often
burdened by the advising and counseling that accompany
their role as a member of a visible minority.

A second reason for encouraging the diversification of faculty and staff is that diversification is an important symbol to
students from these groups about their own futures and about
the institution's commitment to them. Third, diversification
of the campus community creates a more comfortable environment for students as well as for faculty and staff. The strains
suffered by students also exist for faculty and staff members
who represent diverse groups. These individuals assume the
burden of being spokespersons, mentors, support persons,
and symbols, while also trying to perform to rigorous professional standards. At the same time, they may endure the
same kind of loneliness and insensitivities also experienced
by students (Blackwell 1988; Olivas 1988; Smith 1980).

The last two reasons for the importance of a diversified faculty and staff relate to benefits to the institution. Diversifica-

tion of the faculty and staff is likely to contribute to what is taught, how it is taught, and what is important to learn, contributions that are vital to the institution. Faculty trained in traditional pedagogy and in traditional methodologies often find it difficult to fundamentally change courses and curricula. Diversification of the faculty and staff make it easier, because the likelihood is greater for the introduction of different perspectives and approaches and for many more opportunities for professional collaboration. People like administrators and faculty in decision-making positions who have had their own experiences with aspects of institutional life that create barriers or even alienate students offer the institution an invaluable service by providing their perspectives on potential problem areas. It should be remembered, however, that no single individual can represent any more than his or her own perspective or be sensitive to all the issues, needs, and concerns of each disparate group that has been described. An African-American faculty member, for example, cannot reflect all the issues of a disabled or a Latino student. Thus, what is needed is true diversity. Fifth, a diverse faculty and staff reflect one measure of institutional success for an educational institution in a pluralistic society. As long as the leadership of our institutions contains only token representation of persons from diverse backgrounds, institutions will not be able to claim that the goals for society or our educational institutions have been achieved.

Thus, the issue of diversity in faculty and staff assumes direct as well as indirect importance for campus efforts. While these efforts are important for students from those groups, they are also important for the institution. Concern is great, however, that being able to achieve this goal in the near future is highly unlikely (Blackwell 1988; Sudarkasa 1987; Valverde 1988; Wilson 1987a). The lack of growth in higher education over this past decade and the increased use of part-time faculty have combined to produce fewer opportunities for faculty and staff advancement. Now, projections for openings in the next decade are more optimistic, but it is almost universally recognized that the lack of retention and the lack of attractiveness in pursuing advanced degrees for today's and yesterday's undergraduates threaten institutional goals for increasing the hiring of more women and minorities (Blackwell 1988). If the presence of a truly diversified faculty and staff is critical, this situation jeopardizes institutional efforts.

It is important to note that the barrier to diversification is not simply an issue of numbers. Availability of individuals to assume these positions is clearly a problem. Evidence suggests, however, that institutions are also having difficulty retaining faculty and staff of different backgrounds for the same reasons they have had problems retaining students. The current revolving-door pattern is an extravagant waste of human resources and a major obstacle to change. Efforts to retain and develop staff and graduate students already within the institution are therefore as important as increasing the pool of applicants to the institution.

Mission and Values
As indicated earlier, some of the values rooted in the academic tradition are now coming into question. Issues of values are not easily identified, discussed, or dealt with. Given the literature on organizational effectiveness, however, it is probably very important to identify those values that are central to the institution's mission and those that are not. It is also critical that this discussion be held in such a way that traditional assumptions may be open to question. Two sets of values are frequently cited as important: competition/cooperation and individualism/concern for community. The increasing evidence on the effectiveness of cooperative learning, for example, suggests that traditional structures that encourage competitiveness may be counterproductive to the institution and to all students (Astin 1987; Palmer 1987). Rather than being viewed as a threat to institutional quality, such changes may well turn out to improve institutional effectiveness. Discussions about individualism and community touch not only on matters of importance to a number of ethnic and racial groups but also on the increasing concern about narcissism and unethical behavior in society (Harris, Silverstein, and Andrews 1989; McIntosh 1989; Minnich 1989). Have we gone too far in encouraging competitive and highly individualistic practices at the expense of concern for the community and at the expense of good learning?

Questions about values emerge at all levels of the institution. Perhaps one of the most challenging has to do with the ways in which students perceive that the values and perspectives they bring with them to the academic community are not appreciated and may even put them into conflict with institutional norms and behaviors. At its worst, students may perceive that they must abandon the values of their own cultures or background to succeed (Ogbu 1978). The resulting phenomenon of alienation is contradictory to the central role being given to the importance of involvement in one's education and with the institution.

The question of values also extends to how the campus functions and to the norms and expectations for performance. As has been suggested in this monograph, grading practices, decision making, approaches to learning, residence hall life styles, dress, and interpersonal manners are very much affected by values and by background. Creating a campus environment in which one is free to discuss these issues and in which one can create alternative practices can be difficult. The overall pattern of teaching practices in higher education, for example, has never adequately reflected what we know about learning. Large lecture classes, lack of immediate feedback, multiple choice tests, and so on do not reflect the necessary variety in pedagogy for adequate learning (Smith 1983). One might conjecture that as long as students could succeed despite this kind of teaching and as long as one did not care about those who did not succeed, we did not need to connect teaching with learning. Now those conditions must change. Fewer and fewer students succeed. To connect teaching with learning requires knowing about students, knowing about the subject matter, and knowing about conducive environments for learning. Perhaps because of their marginal status, more of these issues are being raised today as they relate to nontraditional students. Just one example of alternative forms of pedagogy is described in *Women's Ways of Knowing* (Belenky et al. 1986). Despite methodological issues about the study's ability to generalize about gender, the report does vividly describe a group of women's preference for "connected" learning. The authors describe connected learning as an interactive experience in which involvement facilitates learning. In this form of learning, empathy, care, and understanding are viewed as important parts of the process of making judgments. Class participation, collaborative projects, and students' contributing to one another's views would be seen as critical. In contrast, the values implicit in many traditional forms of pedagogy are isolation, cynicism, and competition.

Areas of new inquiry, however, are not always well received, particularly if they are not in the accepted tradition of one's colleagues or institution (Pearson, Shavlik, and Touchton

1989). Many have viewed feminist scholarship and ethnic studies, for example, as peripheral to the curriculum and as subjects of nonserious inquiry. Moreover, some view such scholarship as contributing to the weakening of the curriculum (Bloom 1987). The issues involved go to the heart of such questions as what constitutes a good education, what we mean by quality and how we evaluate it, and the appropriate methodologies in the search for truth. For faculty members interested in asking new questions in new areas, the risk can be great unless those areas are already seen as legitimate or unless they themselves have the status to alter approaches in their fields. And it can be very difficult for those who represent minorities in the decision-making process.

Institutions face a challenge in differentiating between those values and goals that facilitate learning and serve the institution's mission and those values that leave some groups on the margin. At the same time, it is important to be open to new ways of accomplishing goals. Evidence on the benefits of cooperative learning for all students, for example, suggests that traditional structures that build in competition may be counterproductive. Such environments may be detrimental to most students. Values and the clarification of assumptions about values are at the heart of the issue of diversity.

Dealing with Conflict
Even the most superficial analysis of what is happening on many college campuses suggests that conflict is either openly present or just under the surface. Some degree of conflict would be expected when individuals and groups from diverse backgrounds try to come together in an institutional setting (Jones 1987). While increased numbers may be more comfortable to a member of a minority group, they may be more threatening to a member of the majority. Thus, conflict may be intensified on many campuses as they become more diverse or more explicit in their efforts to diversify. A look at the literature on intergroup relations suggests moreover that the conditions are present for conflict, given the competitive environment, unequal status of individuals and groups, frustration caused by hostile environments, and perceptions of unresponsiveness by some and favoritism by others and given that little exists to bring groups together in meaningful contact (Amir 1969; Gamson, Peterson, and Blackburn 1980). Building on the literature of cultural pluralism,

we can expect conflict when desirable values are incompatible. Campuses, for example, are struggling with having to choose between setting desirable standards for speech and behavior and supporting rights of free speech given in the First Amendment (*Stanford Observer* 1989). Yet the existence of conflict may be a good sign that the institution is grappling with many of these issues and is in the process of fundamental change. Indeed, a very significant study of the patterns of adaptation that occur in institutions dealing with issues of diversity suggests that conflict may be part of the process that will assist institutions to identify essential changes (Skinner and Richardson 1988). Conflict can therefore be a pathway to learning (Green 1989).

Though higher education is rooted in a tradition of debate and the free exchange of ideas, it is not clear that dealing with conflict, particularly the kind of conflict apt to become emotional, is one that institutions can deal with very effectively. The conflicts that can emerge from trying to create truly pluralistic environments are uncomfortable and may need to be so. The challenge is to create vehicles for dealing with conflict in an environment that is open to differences. Indeed, a characteristic of many successful campuses has been the creation of strong policies, procedures, and even special programs of mediation and arbitration to recognize the existence of conflict and to use it as a vehicle for learning by the institution (Green 1989).

The Quality of
Interaction on Campus
The body of research cited that reflects the importance of students' involvement with the institution requires an institutional assessment about involvement, how students can become involved, the level of interaction among students and between students and faculty, and the general climate of the campus for involvement. The literature on intergroup relations that suggests the need for students and faculty to participate together in meaningful and important work also supports the iinvolvementf involvement. While residential campuses and smaller institutions have more natural potential to develop involvement, the challenge is present for all institutions. Many campuses use mentor programs, programmatic efforts at the college and departmental levels within the university, residence halls, and athletic programs to build communities of

involved students and faculty. For large public institutions, the challenging question is whether meaningful learning communities can be developed that benefit from diversity.

Educating for Diversity

As institutions begin to evaluate the quality of climate for diversity, one inevitable discussion centers around the role of the educational process and in particular the role of the curriculum (Slaughter 1988). Many more institutions are beginning to articulate a commitment to educate students for living in a pluralistic world and to create environments that embrace diversity. The content of the curriculum insofar as it serves these goals, the styles of teaching, and the modes of assessment are all being evaluated. Schools like Stanford and the University of California–Berkeley have now moved to require that all students develop some familiarity with the diversity of American cultures and with issues of race, class, and gender. Curricular transformation involves the same kind of developmental process as institutional transformation in moving from courses that address the voids in the curriculum to efforts to ask new questions that more naturally embrace the pluralism of perspectives in the field (McIntosh 1989).

The role of pedagogy is very important to this aspect of education. Recognizing that groups and individuals may learn in different ways requires rethinking the ways in which teaching occurs. The increasing community of students with learning disabilities has focused attention on this issue, but the discussion touches on the literature concerning the adult learner, racial and ethnic groups, and women as well. In other words, it touches on more than a majority of all students.

The issue of assessment is another component of this educational challenge. Not only are the goals for assessment ambiguous in terms of the kinds of learning being evaluated; significant questions also exist about many of the forms of assessment now in place. For example, for those with learning disabilities, multiple choice, time-limited tests may be invalid indicators of learning. The controversy concerning the role of standardized tests for women and minorities reflects similar concerns about the validity of present testing approaches. Without valid indicators of learning, underestimating the performance of many populations of students is a significant risk. This controversy is being highlighted by court challenges to the means of awarding New York State scholarships to women and by criticisms of the national movement to require examinations for teachers (Duran 1986; National Center 1989).

The Perceived Conflict between Access and Quality

The continuing message that a fundamental conflict exists between issues of access to the institution and quality is perhaps the most disturbing indication that present institutional approaches to diversity are inadequate (Adolphus 1984; Birnbaum 1988; Mingle 1987; Rendon and Nora 1987; Skinner and Richardson 1988; Stewart 1988). Given the number of national studies concerned about the effectiveness and quality of higher education and the call for increasing standards, the higher education community needs to carefully and thoughtfully address this apparent conflict.

Much of the discussion about improving institutional quality focuses on perceptions about the quality of the students being admitted and concern about lowering standards, although these perceptions can also be found in discussions about hiring and retaining faculty and staff (Gamson 1978; Mingle 1987; Peterson et al. 1978; Willie and McCord 1972). There is reason to believe that the questions being asked and the assumptions being made result in an inappropriate conflict between these two central values. Several important points must be made:

- The concern about the preparation of students, while affecting many minority students, is *not* a minority problem. While the impact of poor preparation on those who come from disadvantaged backgrounds is more devastating, declining preparation of students is a national issue affecting virtually all schools and all students. Indeed, most poorly prepared students are white (SHEEO 1987).
- The concern that the admission of many minority groups represents a lowering of test scores ignores the fact that the goals of higher education with regard to admissions have always reflected different levels of preparation among its students. Even the most highly selective institutions have sought diversity in geography, artistic and athletic talent, and leadership among its students rather than populations of perfect GPAs and SATs. With these types of diversity, quality was discussed hardly at all because the educational community and the public understood that quality presumably embraced the con-

tributions of those with different strengths. Moreover, it was widely recognized that grades and test scores could not define all that was needed for success in academics and the community. The value of diversity when it comes to students that differ markedly from the majority seems to be recognized far less, however.

- Much of the evidence concerning the tension between quality and diversity rests on lower standardized scores. As indicated elsewhere, serious questions exist about the predictive validity and the power of these instruments for women, for many minorities, and for those with learning disabilities (Duran 1986; Grubb 1986; Morris 1979; National Center 1989; Sedlacek 1986; Thomas 1981; Wilson 1980). The same could be said for learning assessment programs that rely on these kinds of measures. Changing measures of assessment does not mean lowering standards for learning. Indeed, one characteristic of institutions described earlier as successful is that they set high standards and expectations. We are challenged to develop adequate assessment programs and to avoid relying on inadequate programs that, because of expediency, have the effect of diminishing the evidence of performance for particular groups. Though assessment takes a different form for faculty and staff, concern exists that many institutions do not know how to evaluate the quality of scholarship or performance of those from different faculty groups as well.

- The problem about quality also involves how we define success in school and a student's capacity to learn. If we assume that only one way to learn is correct and at the same time place individuals in environments that are only marginally dedicated to their success, we are setting up whole groups of students for failure. Early evidence focused attention on academic preparation as the most significant factor in achievement, leading many researchers to conclude that academic success is a function of preparation, not race (Richardson and Bender 1987). As this monograph has suggested, however, to the degree that issues of racism, sexism, homophobia, and the general presence of an alienating environment also affect performance, then lack of performance cannot be focused entirely on the student. All too often we have assumed the institution's perfection and students' incompetence.

Care must be exercised in how we teach, about the environment in which teaching takes place, and about how we assess learning.

Numerous references in the literature suggest that the fundamental predisposition of higher education has been to maintain homogeneity and to adapt only when necessary (Morris 1979; Verdugo 1986). A critical example of it may be occurring now in the discussions about whether some institutions have set limits on access for Asian-American students because they are "overrepresented" in the student body. The credibility of higher education's commitment to quality and diversity is weakened when access of Asian-Americans is limited in the name of diversity and access of African-American and Latino students is limited in the name of quality. The net result of both is to perpetuate homogeneity.

If these two concepts—diversity and quality—remain in conflict, the challenge of diversity will not be met. The questions once again are whether the conflict is real and whether we are asking the right questions. When quality is measured in one way only, conflict between quality and diversity is created (Madrid 1988). The implications are that we can broaden our understanding about quality without diluting expectations for learning or for the curriculum. The institution will need to carefully evaluate its standards, its performance criteria, and the climate in which learning occurs, however.

The Changing Climate

At the same time that institutions that genuinely wish to change face significant challenges, other forces facilitate a recognition of the need for change. As troubling as some of the incidents of racial harassment and sexual harassment have been, they have served to bring to the forefront the nature and depth of some of the problems within the community of higher education. Some institutions have begun to study themselves, listening to the experiences of their staff, students, and faculty while acknowledging the need for change. Many institutions, including some of the more prestigious ones, are now leading the way in their efforts to address some of these issues. At the same time, awareness is growing at the national level that major public policy and social implications are involved. Some of the recent national commissions on the achievements of minorities have been both urgent and eloquent in their calls for change and action.

Changing student demographics and the increased voice that students and staff can find in influencing institutional policy have facilitated the awareness of a need for change. It has combined with continuing institutional concern for enrollments to put students in a more influential position than they have been in during other times. This is now a time of increasing student activism. Over the next decade as large numbers of faculty retire and larger numbers of students enter the collegiate generation, we can anticipate a shift in institutional priorities from a concern for enrollment to a concern about hiring faculty, and it may well shift the focus away from the quality of students' experience to the quality of the faculty's experience (Bowen and Schuster 1986; Smith 1988). The improved environment for faculty, their salaries, and their hiring may assist in attracting more minorities and women to faculty positions. Some evidence suggests, for example, that it may already be occurring. While the overall numbers of minority Ph.D.s has declined in recent years, the number has actually increased for minority women (Coyle and Bae 1987).

An organizational approach to diversity has significance for virtually all institutions regardless of the diversity within their student bodies, for it acknowledges the importance of diversity for society and for its future. The reality of demographic shifts is such that Hawaii's "minority" student enrollment is 66.4 percent and Maine's is 3.8 percent. The approach to educating for all forms of diversity—minorities, women, disabled, adult learners, and part-time learners—and the importance of educating all students to live in a pluralistic world are as relevant to Maine as they are for Hawaii, however.

By creating an organization that can deal with diversity and by taking a comprehensive approach to diversity, institutions will find themselves less fragmented in dealing with the numbers of groups with special needs. It will then be more likely that the special needs and perspectives of any number of groups will be more easily accommodated. Moreover, an institution that organizes for diversity will derive many benefits from this approach, not the least of which is the increased capacity to respond to change (Weick 1979). Other opportunities are present as well:

- Revitalizing the curriculum;
- Developing new approaches to policy and organization;

- Modeling the development and growth of "global villages";
- Increasing dialogue and thus success concerning the characteristics of the environment that foster good teaching and learning;
- Creating an environment that appreciates the ways in which difference contributes to education;
- Clarifying the values that are essential to the academic mission and to the creation of community;
- Benefiting from the diversity of teaching approaches;
- And for students, particularly but not only in residential institutions, experiencing the excitement and opportunities to learn from diversity.

In other words, opportunity is greater for much enhanced institutional success and quality.

ASSESSMENT AND IMPLICATIONS

While the challenge of diversity is indeed a national challenge, no clearly marked paths are present to creating educational organizations prepared for this process, given the complexities involved in the concept itself and in human and organizational behavior in general. Nevertheless, consistencies emerge from a wide-ranging set of literatures suggesting some of the steps needed.

If the perspective of several decades can provide a single prevailing lesson from such changes, however, it is that to simply "add and stir" is not enough.

Institutional Assessment
Information is an important element in efforts to create change and to assess the need for change. One of the important initial strategies that can be applied in an institution is an assessment in which all aspects of the college or university are evaluated and can serve as a point of reference. A fundamental question frames the assessment: How is the institution doing with respect to diversity?

Because the effectiveness of research is critically related to its design, an institutional audit needs to be sure:

- That generalizations across groups are not made until the validity of such groups is confirmed;
- That the perspectives of a diverse set of constituencies and groups are involved in the design and interpretation of the results;
- That the instruments used to collect data, whether surveys, interviews, or tests, are checked for their validity and appropriateness for the campus and its constituencies and that, where possible, multiple methods are used;
- That the aspects of campus life and individual and group characteristics studied are inclusive enough to tap a broad range of issues.

Appendix A lists some of the questions that can be asked in assessing an institution's status with regard to creating an involving environment. It is by no means complete but might provide the basis for an audit guide. *Minorities on Campus* (Green 1989) provides additional questions to broaden the focus.

Research
The need for continued research on diversity in higher education is great. Efforts to identify successful programs that may serve as models for other institutions are very important. The use of national data bases, not only to track students but also

to identify institutional characteristics that facilitate success, provides important perspectives. Studies addressing institutional characteristics, however, must move beyond measures of selectivity and resources to ensure that a broader range of institutional qualities is addressed. We also need to know more about the varieties of ways in which students can be involved and how, if at all, those ways differ among specific populations. A parallel need exists, however, to track the presence and retention of faculty and staff and to look at the institutional experiences of those individuals, not only at the professional level but also at the graduate level. The Council of Graduate Schools (1986) has called for such efforts because of the centrality of faculty and staff for the efforts being considered.

A profound need also exists for greater dialogue concerning the results of empirical studies and for synthesis of results that address both theoretical and applied questions. Part of this dialogue could entail efforts to clarify apparent contradictions so that accurate conclusions can be drawn or so that further research could be developed to clarify these differences. The array of studies available that address similar questions with different methodologies and analyses and all too often reach different conclusions limits the role of the scholar and the researcher in contributing to what is actually occurring in our institutions. The loss is significant not only for educational research but also for effective institutional change.

Because institutions vary in their mission, size, complexity, and makeup, the need continues for institutional research on a number of topics that will allow individual institutions to assess their own success in educating students from widely diverse backgrounds as well as the climate of the institution for these students, for faculty and staff, and for more traditional students. Institutional research on who comes, who stays, students' satisfaction, factors associated with retention and graduation, and alumni perceptions can be very helpful in identifying issues and in creating a climate for change (Smith 1982). Great care must be exercised in framing questions for research, however, so that "deficit" models are not reintroduced.

Coordination among Sectors
Some of the data on educational preparation continue to reinforce the importance of quality preparation in kindergarten

through grade 12 to students, to higher education, and to society as a whole. Traditionally, higher education has not directly addressed these issues except through schools of education. This review reinforces the degree of self-interest that higher education should have in issues of precollegiate education. Clearly, higher education cannot address all these issues on its own, but it is responsible for training the teachers and educators who run schools and has an important role in the nature of school systems and in the importance given to the educational profession. Higher education also produces the scholars for future generations of faculty. Moreover, the standards set for entrance and for assessment have an impact throughout the school years. The presidents of Stanford and Harvard are two leading educators who have acknowledged the importance of the role higher education should take in this effort. The nature of the education all students receive concerning issues of diversity can have a major impact throughout the educational system.

Additionally, in states where community colleges assume a significant role in the education of students—and in particular, minority and adult students—articulation between two-year and four-year institutions must be strengthened. This priority is addressed in California, which is actively attempting to address this issue through the development of a revised master plan for higher education in the state (Joint Committee 1988). Following up on students' progress, early intervention, articulation of courses, and coordinated student services are all important features of this effort (Cohen 1988; Donovan, Schaier-Peleg, and Forer 1987; Richardson and Bender 1987). Gathering data is a critical element, though trying to assess the retention and transfer rates from two-year institutions to four-year institutions is a challenge, given the diverse reasons students have for attending community colleges.

State higher education executive officers have developed an important report outlining the particularly significant role that states can play in setting policies and expectations to facilitate institutional and cooperative responses. In addition to financial support, programmatic support, and policy, states have important roles in the design and implementation of effective programs to gather data (Callan 1988; SHEEO 1987).

National Issues
In addition to the national studies that clarify, study, and bring attention to the challenges of diversity, a need exists for sup-

port in encouraging students to enter teaching and those fields where women and minorities have traditionally been underrepresented. Sufficient evidence suggests that previous national, corporate, and foundation efforts to encourage students to enter graduate and professional schools have been successful. That need is emerging once again as higher education prepares for a new wave of challenges and opportunities presented through the attrition of faculty hired during the growth of the sixties (Council of Graduate Schools 1986). Related to these kinds of programs is the need to focus once again on financial assistance so that students can more reasonably choose programs appropriate to their goals. They can involve direct assistance as well as programs that forgive loan obligations for students going into certain fields, such as teaching.

Costs and Commitment

Some students are very much affected by issues of cost. Yet federal and state funding of financial aid has decreased during the last 10 years, and many institutions have seen the percentage of their resources allocated to financial aid growing larger and faster than any other portion of the budget (Stampen and Fenske 1988). The pressures on institutional budgets and national pressure to limit the increase in growth for the costs of higher education place significant strain on institutions to limit spending. To the degree that some of the changes needed, such as increased financial aid to minority students or part-time students, add to costs, the changes will be slowed.

Perhaps one of the greatest challenges presented is the need for sustained commitment and effort. The need for change is urgent, but institutional change will not be easy or quick. With equal parts of dismay and cynicism, numbers of writers observe that higher education's concerns for such issues run in cycles. Indeed, "unless we recognize the systemic nature of persistent racial inequalities, progress . . . may never be more than marginal and episodic" (Morris 1979, p. 269). Others suggest that it is only in response to a crisis that institutions or those involved in public policy will respond. The implication is that when the crisis ends, the commitment also ends (Adolphus 1984). While many are calling it a crisis, the nature of the change needed will no doubt require sustained commitment. "What is needed is a level of commitment such that the risk of retreat is forever banished" (SHEEO 1987, p. 12).

Leadership

While some authors are inclined to debate the importance of leadership in creating change, studies to date reflect the importance of institutional leadership in creating a climate for change and in achieving change. Leadership is required not only to set explicit goals and provide the resources for change but also to frame relevant questions and set the tone for the resulting discussions. For example, the dichotomy between quality and diversity needs to be eliminated so that the necessary discussions can occur in a climate that does not assume that being different is synonymous with being inferior. Energetic leadership will be required to achieve the diversity in faculty and staff that is essential to success.

Throughout the literature is the implication that some of the prevailing attitudes and values in higher education not only create a chilly climate but also may actually impede learning for many more than a minority of students. Indeed, it impedes learning for the majority. Addressing issues of cooperation versus competition and individualism versus community may result in a far healthier community and a far stronger educational system. These issues, however, require careful analysis and discussion. Sensitive and educated leadership will be required.

Conclusion

Twenty years ago a concerted effort was begun to change the shape of American higher education. In that it resulted in changes in the programs and curricula of the academy and in the makeup of its students, faculties, and staffs, these efforts have been successful. If the perspective of several decades can provide a single prevailing lesson from such changes, however, it is that to simply "add and stir" is not enough. Whether or not the melting pot will be the metaphor for pluralism, embracing diversity in all its obvious and subtle forms will be its necessary ingredient. Nearly 400 years ago, the poet John Donne observed that the loss of one person represents more than the loss of one small piece of humanity; it represents a loss to all of humanity. Donne's ancient bell tolls still, for clearly the issues of diversity have significance beyond those of the disenfranchised, beyond communities that exclude rather than include. If higher education is to meet the needs of all of its constituents, these issues must be confronted—not just because they are important to a special group but because they are vital to all institutions and the nation.

INSTITUTIONAL CHARACTERISTICS

- **Makeup of the student body**
  What is the demographic makeup of the student body at both
  the undergraduate and graduate levels in terms of racial and
  ethnic minorities, gender, age, part-time or full-time status, students with disabilities? What issues of preparation are evident
  in the student body? What is the retention rate of each subpop-
  ulation in relation to the whole and to each other? How do graduation rates compare?
  What information is available about the factors associated with
  success? What is changing and how are these changes viewed
  from the perspective of the various campus constituencies? In
  what ways does the institution involve students? Does the leadership among students reflect the diversity on campus?

- **Makeup of the faculty and staff**
  What level of diversity is present within the faculty and staff?
  Do significant gaps exist between the character of the student
  body and the character of the faculty and administration? Is it
  clear that standards for recruitment and promotion are fair and
  can be evaluated appropriately? Are faculty and staff who represent nontraditional groups concentrated in special programs
  or are they well represented throughout the institution? How
  successful is the institution in retaining and promoting such faculty and staff? What are the levels of satisfaction for the faculty
  and staff as a whole? For various subgroups? Does the leadership
  of the organization exhibit diversity?

- **The physical and visual environment**
  What, if any, physical barriers exist? To what degree do the archi-
  tecture, use of space, and art communicate a value of diversity?

- **Special programs**
  Have the special needs of specific groups been audited? What
  is needed for whom? How successful have institutional programmatic efforts been? Are sufficient resources available to provide
  necessary support to students so they can succeed? What role
  does financial aid play in students' retention and performance?
  Are financial aid policies flexible enough to meet the needs of
  diverse student groups?

- **Psychosocial environment**
  What are the expectations for success in the environment?
  What is the level of faculty, administrative, and board support
  for individuals and for programs? What are the attitudes within
  the campus community about different groups and about diversity? Is the population comfortable with differences? Do any
  explicit or implicit values alienate rather than involve particular

groups? What are the ways in which the institution involves or fails to involve all members of the community in the institution? What are the levels of satisfaction among diverse faculty, student, staff, and board groups? What are the patterns of interaction among students and between students and faculty? What feedback do alumni have about their experiences in the institution?

- **The curriculum**
  To what degree are students aware of the diversity in their institution and in the country? How knowledgeable are they about that diversity and about the cultures, histories, and situations of those from whom they differ? To what degree does the curriculum reflect the variety of new scholarship relating to diversity? (In some institutions, the curriculum will never be comprehensive, but being carefully selective can reflect a knowledge of and respect for diversity.) What are the educational goals for all students? What evidence exists that the institution is successful in educating for diversity? How does the institution accommodate a variety of learning styles? Are any particular values required for success? What means of assessment are currently used or considered? What barriers exist to success for each student?

- **Administrative practices**
  Have policies been carefully scrutinized and enforced for their efforts to include, not exclude? Are inappropriate behaviors dealt with decisively? To what degree does the organizational structure involve members of diverse constituencies? Have tangible and visible efforts been made to ensure that decision making at all levels and in all areas reflects the diversity in the community? How successful have recruitment and *retention* of faculty and staff been? Does a program exist to encourage the professional development of faculty and staff at all levels? Does an ongoing program of research exist to assess the institution's effectiveness and success in responding to diversity? What means are available to resolve differences among campus groups and to deal with conflict as a community?

- **Leadership**
  Do visible and tangible signs of leadership focus on organizational responses to diversity? How is the presence of diversity perceived—as a contribution to the scholarly community or as a detraction? Are faculty rewarded for their successes in educating a wide range of students? Do those in leadership positions within the institution, students, faculty, staff, and board bring diverse perspectives to their roles?

REFERENCES

The Educational Resources Information Center (ERIC) Clearinghouse on Higher Education abstracts and indexes the current literature on higher education for inclusion in ERIC's data base and announcement in ERIC's monthly bibliographic journal, *Resources in Education* (RIE). Most of these publications are available through the ERIC Document Reproduction Service (EDRS). For publications cited in this bibliography that are available from EDRS, ordering number and price code are included. Readers who wish to order a publication should write to the ERIC Document Reproduction Service, 3900 Wheeler Avenue, Alexandria, Virginia 22304. (Phone orders with VISA or MasterCard are taken at 800/227-ERIC or 703/823-0500.) When ordering, please specify the document (ED) number. Documents are available as noted in microfiche (MF) and paper copy (PC). If you have the price code ready when you call EDRS, an exact price can be quoted. The last page of the latest issue of *Resources in Education* also has the current cost, listed by code.

Adolphus, Stephen, ed. 1984. *Equality Postponed.* New York: CEEB.

Allen, Walter. 1982. "Undergraduate Survey of Black Undergraduate Students Attending Predominantly White, State-Supported Universities." ED 252 615. 19 pp. MF–01; PC–01.

———. 1986. "Gender and Campus Race Differences in Black Student Academic Performance, Racial Attitudes, and College Satisfaction." Atlanta: Southern Education Foundation. ED 268 855. 123 pp. MF–01; PC–05.

———. 1987. "Black Colleges vs. White Colleges. *Change* 19(3): 28.

———. 1988a. "The Education of Black Students on White College Campuses: What Quality the Experience." In *Toward Black Student Equality in American Higher Education, edited by M. Nettles. New York: Greenwood Press.*

———. *1988b. "Improving Black Student Access and Achievement in Higher Education." Review of Higher Education* 11(4): 403–16.

Allen, Walter, Gerald Gurin, and Marvin W. Peterson. May 1988. "Black Students in White Institutions: The Effectiveness of Different Institutional Responses." Unpublished proposal. Ann Arbor: University of Michigan, Center for the Study of Higher Education, Center for Afro-American Studies.

Allport, Gordon. 1954. *The Nature of Prejudice.* Cambridge, Mass.: Addison-Wesley.

Amir, Y. 1969. "Contact Hypothesis in Ethnic Relations." *Psychological Bulletin* 71(5): 314–42.

Anderson, T. 1987. "Black Encounters of Racism and Elitism in White Academe: A Critique of the System." *Journal of Black Studies* 18(3): 259–72.

Arbeiter, Solomon. 1987. "Black Enrollment." *Change* 19(3): 14–19.

Arciniega, Thomas A. 1985. "Hispanics and Higher Education: A CSU Imperative." California State Univ., Office of the Chancellor.

Armstrong-West, Suzan, and Magdalena H. de la Teja. 1988. "Social and Psychological Factors Affecting the Retention of Minority Students." In *From Survival to Success,* edited by Terrell and Wright. NASPA Monograph Series Vol. 9. HE 022 232. 149 pp. MF–01; PC–06.

Asamen, J., and G.L. Berry. 1987. "Self-Concept, Alienation, and Perceived Prejudice: Implications for Counseling Asian- Americans." *Journal of Multicultural Counseling and Development* 15(4): 146–60.

Asch, A. 1984. "The Experience of Disability: A Challenge for Psychology." *American Psychologist* 39: 529–36.

Asian-American Student Association. 1984. "Asian-American Admissions at Brown University." *Integrated Education* 22(1–3): 31–41.

Astin, Alexander W. 1975. *Preventing Students from Dropping Out.* San Francisco: Jossey-Bass.

———. 1982. *Minorities in American Higher Education: Recent Trends, Current Prospects, and Recommendations. San Francisco: Jossey-Bass.*

———. 1984. *"A Look at Pluralism in the Contemporary Student Population." NASPA Journal* 21(3): 2–11.

———. 1985. "Involvement: The Cornerstone of Excellence." *Change* 17(4): 35–39.

———. 1987. "Competition or Cooperation." *Change* 19(5): 12–19.

Astin, Alexander, Kenneth Green, and William Korn. 1987. *The American Freshman: Twenty-Year Trends.* Los Angeles: UCLA. ED 279 279. 225 pp. MF–01; PC not available EDRS.

Astin, Helen W., and C.P. Burciaga. 1981. *Chicanos in Higher Education: Progress and Attainment.* Los Angeles: Higher Education Research Institute. ED 226 690. 179 pp. MF–01; PC–08.

Babbit, Charles E., Harold J. Bruback, and Myron A. Thompson. 1975. "Organizational Alienation among Black College Students: A Comparison of Three Educational Settings." *Journal of College Student Personnel* 16" 53–56.

Banks, J.A. 1981. *Education in the 80s: Multiethnic Education.* Washington, D.C.: NEA. ED 204 192. 188 pp. MF–01; PC not available EDRS.

Barbarin, O.A. 1981. *Institutional Racism and Community Competence.* Bethesda, Md.: NIMH. ED 222 605. 254 pp. MF–01; PC–11.

Bauer, W.K. 1981. "Strategies for Recruiting and Retaining the Nontraditional Student." *College Student Personnel* 15(3): 234–38.

Bean, John P., and Barbara S. Metzner. 1985. "A Conceptual Model of Nontraditional Undergraduate Student Attrition." *Review of Educational Research* 55(4): 485–540.

Bechman, B. 1984. *The Black Student's Guide to Colleges*. Providence, R.I.: Bechman-Harris.

Beckham, Barry. 1988. "Strangers in a Strange Land: The Experience of Blacks on White Campuses." *Educational Record* 68(4), 69(1): 74–78.

Belenky, Mary F., Blythe M. Clinchy, Nancy Goldberger, and J.M. Tarule. 1986. *Women's Ways of Knowing*. New York: Basic Books.

Belgrave, F.Z. 1984. "The Effectiveness of Strategies for Increasing Social Interaction of a Physically Disabled Person." *Journal of Applied Social Psychology* 74(2): 147–61.

Bell-Scott, Patricia. 1984. "Black Women's Higher Education: Our Legacy." *Sage* 6(7): 8–11.

Bennett, Christine, and John Bean. 1983. "Explanations of Attrition among Black Students at a Predominantly White Institution." Paper presented at a meeting of the American Educational Research Association, April, Boston, Massachusetts.

Bennett, Christine, and Alton Okinaka. 1984. "Explanations of Black Student Attrition in Predominantly White and Predominantly Black Universities." *Integrated Education* 22(13): 73–80.

Birnbaum, Robert. 1988. "Administrative Commitments and Minority Enrollments: College Presidents' Goals for Quality and Access." *Review of Higher Education* 11(4): 435–58.

Blackwell, James E. 1987. *Mainstreaming Outsiders*. New York: General Hall.

———. 1988. "Faculty Issues: The Impact on Minorities." *Review of Higher Education* 11(8): 417–34.

Blake, Elias. 1987. "Equality for Blacks." *Change* 19(3): 10–13.

Blakely, William. 1987. "Take a Leaf from Joe Poterno: An Interview with William Blakely." *Change* 19(3): 41–43.

Bloom, Allan. 1987. *The Closing of the American Mind*. New York: Touchton.

Bodenkoop, M.S., and M.K. Johansen. 1980. "Do Reentry Women Have Special Needs?" *Psychology of Women Quarterly* 4(4): 591–95.

Bornholdt, Laura. 1987. "Time for a Second Generation Effort." *Change* 19(3): 6–7.

Bowen, Howard, and Jack Schuster. 1986. *American Professors: A National Resource Imperiled*. New York: Oxford Univ. Press.

Bowser, Benjamin P., and Raymond G. Hunt. 1981. *Impacts of Racism on White Americans*. Beverly Hills, Cal.: Sage.

Boyd, W.M. 1982. "The Secret of Minority Retention." *AGB Reports* 24(2): 17–21.

Boyer, Ernest. 1986. *College: The Undergraduate Experience in America.* New York: Carnegie Commission for the Advancement of Teaching.

Braddock, Jomills H. 1978. "Radicalism and Alienation among Black College Students." *Negro Educational Review* 29(1): 4–21.

Braddock, Jomills, and James McPartland. 1988. "Some Cost and Benefit Considerations for Black College Students Attending Predominantly White versus Predominantly Black Universities." In *Toward Black Undergraduate Student Equality in American Higher Education,* edited by M. Nettles. New York: Greenwood Press.

Brown, G.H., N.L. Rosen, and S.T. Hill. 1980. *The Condition of Education for Hispanic Americans.* Washington, D.C.: Center for Education Statistics. ED 188 853. 279 pp. MF–01; PC–12.

Brown, T.H. 1982. "Testimony to the National Commission on Excellence in Education" at a public hearing in Chicago. ED 237 016. 9 pp. MF–01; PC–01.

Bruner, Jerome. 1983. *In Search of Mind: Essays in Autobiography.* New York: Harper & Row.

Burgos-Sasscer, Ruth. 1987. "Empowering Hispanic Students: A Prerequisite Is Adequate Data." *Journal of Educational Equity and Leadership* 7(7): 21–36.

Burrell, L.F. 1980. "Is There a Future for Black Students on Predominantly White Campuses?" *Integrated Education* 18(5–6): 23–27.

California Community Colleges, Chancellor's Office. 1986. *Disabled Students in the California Community Colleges: A Report.* Long Beach: Author.

Callan, Patrick M. 1988. "Minority Degree Achievement and the State Policy Environment." *Review of Higher Education* 11(4): 355–64.

Cardoza, Jana. 1986. "Colleges Alerted: Pay Attention to Minorities—or Risk Future Survival." *ETS Development* 32(2): 8–10.

Carnegie Foundation for the Advancement of Teaching. 1987. "Minority Access: A Question of Equity." *Change* 19(3): 35–39.

Carodo, T.J., and J.A. Mangano. 1982. "The Making and Seeding of RASP: Development and Dissemination of a Model to Ease the Reentry Process of Adult Students in Two-Year Colleges." Paper presented at a meeting of the American Educational Research Association, March. ED 223 307. 32 pp. MF–01; PC–02.

Carter, Deborah, Carol S. Pearson, and Donna Shavlik. 1988. "Double Jeopardy: Women of Color in Higher Education." *Educational Record* 69(1): 86–103.

Carter, Robert T., and William E. Sedlacek. 1984. *Interracial Contact, Background, and Attitudes: Implications for Campus Programs.* Research Report No. 13-84. College Park: Univ. of Maryland. ED 268 422. 15 pp. MF–01; PC–01.

Carter, Robert T., Timothy J. White, and William E. Sedlacek. 1985.

White Students' Attitude toward Black: Implications for Recruitment and Retention. Research Report No. 12-85. College Park: Univ. of Maryland. ED 278 330. 23 pp. MF–01; PC–01.

Carver, C.S., D.C. Glass, and I. Katz. 1978. "Favorable Evaluations of Blacks and the Handicapped: Positive Prejudices, Unconscious Denial, or Social Desirability?" *Journal of Applied Social Psychology* 8: 97–106.

Castaneda, Alfredo. 1974. "Ideological Issues of Assimilation in America." In *Cultural Pluralism,* edited by Edgar G. Epps. Berkeley, Cal.: McCutchan.

Center for Education Statistics. 1986. *Growth in Higher Education Enrollment: 1978 to 1985.* Washington, D.C.: Author. ED 284 471. 15 pp. MF–01; PC–01.

––––––. 1987. *Digest of Education Statistics.* Washington, D.C.: Thomas D. Snyder. ED 282 359. 424 pp. MF–01; PC–17.

Chacon, Maria A., Eleanor G. Cohen, and S. Strover. 1986. "Chicanas and Chicanos: Barriers to Progress." In *Latino College Students,* edited by M.A. Olivas. New York: Teachers College Press.

Chew, Charlene A., and Alan Y. Ogi. 1987. "Asian-American College Student Perspectives." In *Responding to the Needs of Today's Minority Students,* edited by D.J. Wright. New Directions for Student Services No. 38. San Francisco: Jossey- Bass.

Clark, Burton R. 1972. "The Organizational Saga in Higher Education." *Administrative Science Quarterly* 17(2): 178–84.

Claxton, Charles S., and Patricia H. Murrell. 1987. *Learning Styles: Implications for Improving Educational Practices.* ASHE-ERIC Higher Education Report No. 4. Washington, D.C.: Association for the Study of Higher Education. ED 293 478. 116 pp. MF–01; PC–05.

Clewell, B., and M.S. Ficklen. 1986. *Improving Minority Retention in Higher Education: A Search for Effective Institutional Practices.* Princeton, N.J.: Educational Testing Service. ED 299 841. 162 pp. MF–01; PC–07.

Clowes, Darrell A., Dennis E. Hinkle, and John C. Smart. 1986. "Enrollment Patterns in Postsecondary Education, 1961–82." *Journal of Higher Education* 57(2): 121–33.

Cohen, Arthur M. 1988. "Degree Achievement by Minorities in Community Colleges." *Review of Higher Education* 11(4): 383–402.

"The College President: A New Survey by the ACE." 30 March 1988. *Chronicle of Higher Education:* A14.

Commission on Minority Participation in Education and American Life. 1988. *One-third of a Nation.* Washington, D.C.: American Council on Education.

Cope, Robert G., and William Hannah. 1975. *Revolving-Door Colleges: The Causes and Consequences of Dropping Out, Stopping Out, and Transferring.* New York: John Wiley & Sons.

Council of Graduate Schools. 1986. *CGS Task Force on Minorities in Graduate Education.* ED 276 396. 47 pp. MF–01; PC–02.

Courage, R. 1984. "What's Different about Teaching Adult Student Writers?" Paper presented at a meeting of the National Council of Teachers of English, November. ED 259 372. 29 pp. MF–01; PC–02.

Cox, William E., and Catherine C. Jobe. 1988. "Recruiting Wars: Can Higher Education Compete with the Military?" *Educational Record* 68(4)–69(1): 63–69.

Coyle, S., and Yupin Bae. 1987. *Summary Report: 1986 Doctorate Recipients from U.S. Universities.* Washington, D.C.: National Academy Press.

Creange, Renee. 1980. *Student Support Services: Reentry Women Need Them Too.* Washington, D.C.: Association of American Colleges. ED 196 338. 13 pp. MF–01; PC–01.

Cross, K. Patricia, and Helen Astin. 1981. "Factors Affecting Black Student Persistence." In *Black Students in Higher Education,* edited by Gail E. Thoms. Westport, Conn.: Greenwood Press.

Crosson, Patricia H. 1988. "Four-Year College and University Environments for Minority Degree Achievement." *Review of Higher Education* 11(4): 365–82.

Davis, J.E., and M.T. Nettles. 1987. "Academic Profession and Students at Public and Private Historically Black Colleges." Paper presented at a meeting of the Association for the Study of Higher Education. ED 281 462.

de los Santos, A.G. 1986. "Facing the Facts about Mexican America." Paper presented at a meeting of the American Association for Higher Education, March, Washington, D.C. ED 271 081. 21 pp. MF–01; PC–01.

Demetrulias, Diana A., Joan L. Sattler, and Leslie P. Graham. Summer 1982. "How Do You Know When You Are Hungry?: Disabled Students in University Settings." *Journal of NAWDAC* 45: 8–13.

Desjardins, Carolyn. 1989. "The Meaning of Gilligan's Concept of 'Different Voice' for the Learning Environment." In *Educating the Majority: Women Challenge Tradition in Higher Education,* edited by Carol S. Pearson, Donna L. Shavlik, and Judith Touchton. New York: Macmillan.

DiCesare, A., W.E. Sedlacek, and G.C. Brooks. 1972. "Nonintellectual Correlates of Black Student Attrition." *Journal of College Student Personnel* 13: 319–24.

Dinka, F., F. Mazzella, and D.E. Pilant. 1980. "Reconciliation and Confirmation: Blacks and Whites at a Predominantly White University." *Journal of Black Studies* 7(1): 55–76.

Dix, Linda S., ed. 1987. *Minorities: Their Underrepresentation and Career Differentials in Science and Engineering.* Washington, D.C.: National Academy Press. ED 285 751. 174 pp. MF–01; PC–

07.

Donovan, Richard A., Barbara Schaier-Peleg, and Bruce Forer, eds. 1987. *Transfer: Making It Work. A Community College Report.* Washington, D.C.: American Association of Community and Junior Colleges. ED 281 579. 75 pp. MF–01; PC not available EDRS.

Duffy, Yvonne. 1989. "Enhancing the Effectiveness of Postsecondary Education for Women with Disabilities." In *Educating the Majority: Women Challenge Tradition in Higher Education,* edited by Carol S. Pearson, Donna L. Shavlik, and Judith G. Touchton. New York: Macmillan.

Duhon, Rose M. 1986. "Meeting the Needs of Special Populations: Off-Campus Minority Students." Paper presented at a meeting of the Association of Teacher Education, February, Atlanta, Georgia.

Duran, Richard P. 1986. "Prediction of Hispanics' College Achievement." In *Latino College Students,* edited by Michael A. Olivas. New York: Teachers College Press.

Durnell, P.L. 1980. *A Needs Assessment of Nontraditional Women Students at the University of Georgia.* Atlanta: Univ. of Georgia. ED 195 219. 45 pp. MF–01; PC–02.

Edelman, Jacob Murray. 1977. *Political Language: Words that Succeed and Policies that Fail.* New York: Academic Press.

Elam, J.C. 1982. *Black on White Campuses.* Washington, D.C.: National Association for Equal Opportunities in Higher Education.

El-Khawas, Elaine. 1987. *Campus Trends.* Report No. 75. Washington, D.C.: American Council on Education. ED 286 402. 52 pp. MF–01; PC–03.

EppsEpps, Edgar G., ed. 1974. *Cultural Pluralism.* Berkeley, Cal.: McCutchan.

Estrada, Leonardo F. 1988. "Anticipating the Demographic Future." *Change* 20(3): 14–19.

Etzioni, A. 1968. *The Active Society.* New York: Free Press.

Feldman, Kenneth A., and Theodore M. Newcomb. 1969. *The Impact of College on Students.* San Francisco: Jossey- Bass.

Fenderson, D.A. 1984. "Opportunities for Psychologists in Disability Research." *American Psychologist* 39: 524–28.

Fichten, Catherine S. 1986. "Attitudes and Beliefs Which Facilitate or Hamper the Integration of Students with Physical Disabilities in Postsecondary Education." In *Attitudes toward Persons with Disabilities,* edited by H. Yuker. New York: Greenwood Press.

Fields, Cheryl. 1988. "The Hispanic Pipeline: Narrow, Leaking, and Needing Repair." *Change* 20(3): 20–27.

Fiske, Edward B. 1988. "The Undergraduate Hispanic: Juggling Two Cultures." *Change* 20(3): 29–33.

Fleming, Jacqueline. 1984. *Blacks in College.* San Francisco: Jossey-Bass.

Fox, R.N. 1985. "Application of a Conceptual Model of College With-drawal to Disadvantaged Students." Paper presented at a meeting of the American Educational Research Association, April, Chicago, Illinois. ED 257 339. 44 pp. MF–01; PC–02.

Frances, Carol. July/August 1980. "Apocalyptic vs. Strategic Planning." *Change:* 19–44.

Frazier, E. Franklin. 1957. *The Negro in the United States.* New York: Macmillan.

Freedman, Theodore. 1981. "Is Civility on the Campus Threatened?" *Educational Record* 62(3): 51–53.

Fries, Judith E. 1987. *The American Indian in Higher Education: 1975–76 to 1984–85.* Washington, D.C.: Center for Education Statistics. ED 281 693. 39 pp. MF–01; PC–02.

Gamson, Zelda F. 1978. "Programs for Black Students, 1968–1974." In *Black Students on White Campuses: The Impact of Increased Black Enrollment,* edited by M.W. Peterson et al. Ann Arbor: Univ. of Michigan, Institute for Social Research.

Gamson, Zelda, Marvin W. Peterson, and Robert T. Blackburn. 1980. "States in the Response of White Colleges and Universities to Black Students." *Journal of Higher Education* 51: 255–67.

Garza, R.T., and D.B. Nelson. 1973. "A Comparison of Mexican and Anglo-American Student Perceptions of the University Environment." *Journal of College Student Personnel* 14(5): 399–401.

Gillespie, Bonnie. 1983. "Financing Traditionally Black Institutions of Higher Education." Paper presented at the Blacks in Higher Education Conference, April, Washington, D.C. ED 234 113. 33 pp. MF–01; PC–02.

Gittell, Marilyn. 1985. "Reaching the Hard to Reach." *Change* 17(4): 51–60.

Glennen, R.E., D.M. Boxley, and P.J. Farren. 1985. "Impact of Intrusive Advising on Minority Student Retention." *College Student Journal* 19(4): 335.

Goldberg, B., et al. 1985. *Perceived Effects of a Financial Aid Scholarship on Returning Women Students.* Research Report No. 7-85. College Park: Univ. of Maryland. ED 272 088. 9 pp. MF–01; PC–01.

Gordon, M. 1964. *Assimilation in American Life.* New York: Oxford Univ. Press.

Green, Madeleine. 1989. *Minorities on Campus: A Handbook for Enhancing Diversity.* Washington, D.C.: American Council on Education.

Griffith, A.R. 1978. "A Cultural Perspective for Counseling Blacks." *Journal of College Student Personnel* 19: 249–54.

Grubb, Henry J. 1986. "Prediction of College Academic Functioning: Similarities and Differences between Blacks and Whites." Paper presented at a meeting of the Southeastern Psychological Association, March, Kissimmee, Florida.

Gurin, Patricia, and Edgar G. Epps. 1975. *Black Consciousness, Identity, and Achievement*. New York: John Wiley & Sons.

Guyette, S., and C. Heth. 1983. "American Indian Higher Education: Needs and Projections." Paper presented at an annual conference of the American Educational Research Association, April, Montreal, Quebec, Canada. ED 232 810. 28 pp. MF–01; PC–02.

Hall, E.R. 1984. "Minority Students at the University of Wisconsin–Milwaukee: Who Are They and How Are They Doing?" Paper presented at a meeting of the Wisconsin Educational Research Association. ED 249 829. 25 pp. MF–01; PC–01.

———. 1986. "Role Demands and College Experiences of Minority and White Men and Women." Paper presented at an AIR Annual Forum. ED 280 387. 23 pp. MF–01; PC–01.

Hameister, Brenda. 1984. "Orienting Disabled Students." In *Orienting Students to College*, edited by M.L. Upcraft. New Directions for Student Services No. 25. San Francisco: Jossey-Bass.

Harris, Judith, Joann Silverstein, and Dianne Andrews. 1989. "Educating Women in Science." In *Educating the Majority: Women Challenge Tradition in Higher Education*, edited by Carol S. Pearson, Donna L. Shavlik, and Judith G. Touchton. New York: Macmillan.

Hart, P.S. 1984. *Institutional Effectiveness in the Production of Black Baccalaureates*. Southern Education Foundation. ED 246 748. 97 pp. MF–01; PC–04.

Hartnett, R.I. 1970. "Differences in Selected Attitudes and Colleges or between Black Students Attending Traditionally Negro and Traditionally White Institutions." *Sociology of Education* 43(4): 419–36.

Health Resource Center. 1987. *National Clearinghouse on Postsecondary Education for Handicapped Individuals: Resource Directory*. Washington, D.C.: American Council on Education.

Hetherington, C., and G. Hudson. 1981. "Returning Women Students: Independence, Personal Identity, Confidence, and Goal Orientation." *Journal of College Student Personnel* 22(1): 31–36.

Hill, S.T. 1984. "Participation of Black Students in Higher Education: A Statistical Profile." *Integrated Education* 22(1–3): 53–59.

Hilton, Thomas. 1986. "Balanced High School Program More Likely to Lead to Advanced Study." *ETS Development* 32(1): 6.

Hodgkinson, Harold. 1985. *All One System: Demographics of Education, Kindergarten through Graduate School*. Washington, D.C.: Institute of Educational Leadership. ED 261 101. 22 pp. MF–01; PC–01.

Hsia, Jayjia. 1987. "Asian-American Students: Ability, Achievement, and Access to Higher Education." Paper presented at a meeting of the American Educational Research Association, April, Washington, D.C.

———. 1988. "Asian-Americans Fight the Myth of the Super Student." *Educational Record* 68(4)–69(1): 94–97.

Hu, Michael. 1985. "Determining the Needs and Attitudes of Nontraditional Students." *Colleges and Universities* 60(3): 201–9.

Hughes, Rees. 1983. "The Nontraditional Student in Higher Education: A Synthesis of the Literature." *NASPA Journal* 20(3): 51–64.

Hunt, C.L. 1975. "Alternate Patterns of Minority Group Adjustment in the University." *Educational Forum* 39(2): 137–47.

Jaimes, M.A. 1980. "Higher Educational Needs of Indian Students." *Integrated Education* 9(1–2): 7–12.

Jaramillo, Mari Luci. 1988. "Institutional Responsibility in the Provision of Educational Experiences to the Hispanic American Female Student." In *The Broken Web,* edited by T. McKenna and F.I. Ortiz. Encino, Cal.: Floricanto Press.

Jarrow, Jene E. 1987. "Integration of Individuals with Disabilities in Higher Education: A Review of the Literature." *Journal of Postsecondary Education and Disability* 5: 38–57.

Johnson, David W., Roger T. Johnson, and Geoffrey Mariyama. 1983. "Interdependence and Interpersonal Attraction among Heterogeneous and Homogeneous Individuals: A Theoretical Formulation and a Meta-analysis of the Research." *Review of Educational Research* 53(1): 5–54.

Joint Committee for Review of the Master Plan in Higher Education. 1988. "California Faces ... California's Future: Education for Citizenship in a Multicultural Society." Sacramento: Author.

Jones, C.J., L.J. Harris, and W.E. Hanch. 1975. "Differences in the Perceived Sources of Academic Difficulties: Black Students in Predominantly Black and Predominantly White Colleges." *Journal of Negro Education* 44: 519–29.

Jones, W. Terrell. 1987. "Enhancing Minority-White Peer Interactions." In *Responding to the Needs of Today's Minority Students,* edited by D.J. Wright. New Directions for Student Services No. 38. San Francisco: Jossey-Bass.

Kanter, Rosabeth Moss. 1977. *Men and Women of the Corporation.* New York: Basic Books.

Katz, J.H., and Y.A. Ivey. 1977. "White Awareness: The Frontier of Racism Awareness Training." *Personality and Guidance Journal* 55: 485–89.

Kirchner, C., and Z. Simon. 1984. "Blind and Visually Handicapped College Students. Part I: Estimated Number." *Journal of Visual Impairment and Blindness* 78(2): 78–81.

Knowles, M. 1978. *The Adult Learner: A Neglected Species.* Houston: Gulf Publishing.

Konrad, Alison M., and Barbara A. Gutek. 1987. "Theory and Research on Group Composition: Applications to the Status of Women and

Ethnic Minorities." In *Interpersonal Processes of the Claremont Symposium on Applied Social Psychology,* edited by S. Oskamp and S. Spacapan. Beverly Hills, Cal.: Sage.

Korolewicz, M., and A. Korolewicz. 1985. "Effects of Sex and Race on Interracial Dating Preferences." *Psychological Reports* 57: 291–96.

Kraiger, Kurt, and J. Kevin Ford. 1985. "A Meta-analysis of Rater Race Effects in Performance Ratings." *Journal of Applied Psychology* 70(1): 56–65.

Krupnick, C.G. 1985. "Women and Men in the Classroom: Inequality and Its Remedies." *On Teaching and Learning* (May): 18–25.

LaCounta, Deborah Wetsit. 1987. "American Indian Students in College." In *Responding to the Needs of Today's Minority Students,* edited by D.J. Wright. New Directions for Student Services No. 38. San Francisco: Jossey-Bass.

Lang, Marvel. 1987. "Recent Trends in Black Student Retention in Higher Education: A Statistical Synthesis." Paper presented at a meeting of Black Student Retention in Higher Education, November, Tampa, Florida.

Larwood, Laurie, Barbara A. Gutek, and Urs E. Gattiker. 1984. "Perspectives on Institutional Discrimination and Resistance to Change." *Group and Organizational Studies* 9(3): 333–52.

Lasser, Carol, ed. 1987. *Educating Men and Women Together.* Carbondale: Univ. of Illinois.

Lee, John B., M.K. Rotermund, and J.A. Bertselman. 1985. *Student Aid and Minority Enrollment in Higher Education.* Washington, D.C.: American Association of State Colleges and Universities.

Lee, Valerie. 1985. *Access to Higher Education: The Experience of Blacks, Hispanics, and Low SES Whites.* Washington, D.C.: American Council on Education. ED 258 505. 63 pp. MF–01; PC–03.

Le Flore, Fannie. 1982. "Fannie: Claiming an Integrated Experience—The Parties Are All Segregated." *Journal of Education Today* 15(4): 4–5.

Livingston, M.D., and M.A. Stewart. 1987. "Minority Students on a White Campus: Perception Is Truth." *NASPA Journal* 24(3): 40–49.

Loo, Chalsa M., and Garry Rolison. 1986. "Alienation of Ethnic Minority Students at a Predominantly White University." *Journal of Higher Education* 57(1): 59–77.

Lopez, M., and M. Clyde-Synder. 1983. "Higher Education for the Learning-Disabled Students." *NASPA Journal* 20(4): 34–39.

Lunneborg, Patricia, and Clifford E. Lunneborg. 1985. "Student-Centered vs. University-Centered Problems of Minority Students." *Journal of College Student Personnel* 26(3): 224–28.

Lynch, D.O. 1985. "Access, Involvement, and Excellence: A Theoretical Framework." Paper presented at the University of Wisconsin

Multicultural Conference, Milwaukee, Wisconsin. ED 273 233. 12 pp. MF–01; PC–01.

McBay, Shirley. 1986. *The Racial Climate on the MIT Campus.* Boston: Massachusetts Institute of Technology.

McClain, B.R. 1979. "The Need for Black Colleges: A Black Perspective." *Crisis* 86(5): 151–54.

McIntosh, Peggy. 1989. "Curricular Revision: The New Knowledge for a New Age." In *Educating the Majority: Women Challenge Tradition in Higher Education,* edited by Carol S. Pearson, Donna L. Shavlik, and Judith G. Touchton. New York: Macmillan.

McIntyre, J.L. 1981. "Nontraditional Strategies for Nontraditional Students." ED 205 899. 13 pp. MF–01; PC–01.

McKenna, Teresa, and Flora Ortiz, eds. 1988. *The Broken Web.* Encino, Cal.: Floricanto Press.

Madden, M.E., S.M. Woods, S. Dares-Hobbs, and J. Collins. 1987. "Perceived Control and Student Involvement in Campus Activities." *Journal of College Student Personnel* 28(4): 370–71.

Madrozo-Peterson, R., and M. Rodriguez. 1978. "Minority Students' Perceptions of a University Environment." *Journal of College Student Personnel* 19: 259–64.

Madrid, Arturo. 1988. "Diversity and Its Discontents." Paper presented at a national conference of the American Association for Higher Education, March, Washington, D.C.

Mallinckrodt, Brent, and William E. Sedlacek. 1987. "Student Retention and the Use of Campus Facilities by Race." *NASPA Journal* 24(3): 28–32.

Marion, P.B., and E.V. Iovacchini. 1983. "Services for Handicapped Students in Higher Education: An Analysis of National Trends." *Journal of College Student Personnel* 24: 131–37.

Martin, Jane R. 1985. "Becoming Educated: A Journey of Alienation or Integration." *Journal of Education* 167(3): 71–84.

Martinez, Alyce, and William E. Sedlacek. 1983. "Changes in the Social Climate of a Campus over a Decade." *College and University* 58: 254–57.

Maryland State Board for Higher Education. 1981. *Enhancement of Maryland's Predominantly Black Collegiate Institutions.* ED 214 422. 333 pp. MF–01; PC–14.

Masland, Andrew T. 1985. "Organizational Culture in the Study of Higher Education." *Review of Higher Education* 8(2): 157–68.

Maynard, M. 1980. "Can Universities Adapt to Ethnic Minority Students' Needs?" *Journal of College Student Personnel* 21(4): 398–401.

Mick, Lori B. 1985. "Connecting Link between Secondary and Postsecondary Programs for Learning Disabled Persons." *Journal of College Student Personnel* 26(5): 463–65.

Minatoya, Lydia Y., and William E. Sedlacek. 1984. "Assessing Attitudes of White University Students toward Blacks in a Changing Context." *Journal of Nonwhite Concern in Personnel and Guidance* 12: 69–79.

Mingle, James R. 1987. *Focus on Minorities: Trends in Higher Education Participation and Success.* Education Commission of the States/SHEEO. ED 287 404. 50 pp. MF–01; PC–02.

Minnich, Elizabeth. 1989. "From the Circle of the Elite to the World of the Whole." In *Educating the Majority: Women Challenge Tradition in Higher Education,* edited by Carol S. Pearson, Donna L. Shavlik, and Judith G. Touchton. New York: Macmillan.

Morris, Lorenzo. 1979. *Elusive Equality.* Washington, D.C.: Howard Univ. Press.

———. 1981. "The Role of Testing in Institutional Selectivity and Black Access to Higher Education." In *Black Students in Higher Education,* edited by Gail E. Thoms. Westport, Conn.: Greenwood Press.

Myrdal, Gunnar. 1962. *An American Dilemma.* New York: Harper & Row.

National Center for Fair and Open Testing. 1989. *FairTest Examiner* 3(1): 1–3.

Neher, W.W. 1985. "Recruitment and Retention of Minority Students in Small Colleges." ED 259 408. 11 pp. MF–01; PC–01.

Nelms, C. 1982. "Minorities and the Professions." *Action in Teacher Education* 4(2): 47–52.

Nettles, Michael T. 1986. "Black and White Students' College Performance in Majority White and Majority Black Academic Settings." In *Title VI Regulations for Higher Education: Problems and Progress,* edited by J. Williams. New York: Teachers College Press.

———. 1988a. "Black and White Students' Academic Performance in Majority White and Majority Black College Settings." In *Desegregating America's Colleges and Universities,* edited by John B. Williams, III. New York: Teachers College Press.

———. 1988b. *Toward Black Undergraduate Student Equality in American Higher Education.* Westport, Conn.: Greenwood Press.

Nettles, Michael T., and Janet R. Johnson. 1987. "Race, Sex, and Other Factors as Determinants of College Students' Socialization." *Journal of College Student Personnel* 28(6): 512–24.

Nettles, Michael T., A. Robert Thoeny, and Erica J. Gosman. 1986. "Comparative and Predictive Analyses of Black and White Students' College Achievement and Experiences." *Journal of Higher Education* 57: 289–318.

———. 1987. "Racial Differences in College Student Achievement." In *In Pursuit of Equality in Higher Education,* edited by A.S. Pruitt. New York: General Hall.

Nora, Amaury. 1987. "Determinants of Retention among Chicano College Students: A Structural Model." *Research in Higher Edu-*

cation 26(1): 31-57.

Oates, Mary J., and Susan Williamson. 1978. "Women's Colleges and Women Achievers." *Signs: Journal of Women in Culture and Society* 3(4): 795-806.

O'Barr, Jean F. 1989. "Reentry Women in the Academy." In *Educating the Majority: Women Challenge Tradition in Higher Education,* edited by Carol S. Pearson, Donna L. Shavlik, and Judith G. Touchton. New York: Macmillan.

Ogbu, J.J. 1978. *Minority Education and Caste: The American System in Cross-Cultural Perspective.* New York: Academic Press.

Olivas, Michael A. 1986. "Research on Latino College Students: A Theoretical Framework and Inquiry." In *Latino College Students,* edited by Michael A. Olivas. New York: Teachers College Press.

———. 1988. "Latino Faculty at the Border." *Change* 20(3): 6-9.

Oliver, John, and Roland Etcheverry. 1987. "Factors Influencing the Decisions of Academically Talented Black Students to Attend College." *Journal of Negro Education* 56(2): 152-61.

Oliver, M.L., et al. 1985. "Brown and Black in White: The Social Adjustment and Academic Performance of Chicano and Black Students

in a Predominantly White University." *Urban Review* 17(1): 3-23.

Ostar, A.W. July 1985. "Quality and Education in Higher Education." *Higher Education and National Affairs* 34: 7.

Pace, C. Robert. 1984. *Measuring the Quality of College Student Experiences.* Los Angeles: Univ. of California–Los Angeles, Higher Education Research Institute. ED 255 099. 142 pp. MF–01; PC–06.

Palmer, Parker J. 1987. "Community Conflict and Ways of Knowing." *Change* 19(5): 20-25.

Pantages, Timothy J., and Carol F. Creedon. 1978. "Studies of College Attrition: 1950-1975." *Review of Educational Research* 48: 49-101.

Parker, Woodrow M., James Scott, and Anthony Chambers. 1985. "Creating an Inviting Atmosphere for College Students from Ethnic Minority Groups." *Journal of College Student Personnel* 26(1): 82-84.

Pascarella, Ernest T. 1980. "Student-Faculty Informal Contact and College Outcomes." *Review of Educational Research* 50: 545-95.

———. 1985. "Racial Differences in Factors Associated with Bachelor's Degree Completion: A Nine-Year Followup." *Research in Higher Education* 23(4): 351-73.

Pascarella, Ernest T., John C. Smart, and J. Stoecker. 1989. "Race and the Early Status Attainment of Black Students." *Journal of Higher Education* 60(1): 82-107.

Patterson, Aldrich M., and William E. Sedlacek. 1984. "Differences among Minority Student Backgrounds and Attitudes toward a University and Its Services." *Integrated Education* 22(1-3): 95-101.

Patterson, Aldrich M., William E. Sedlacek, and F.W. Perry. 1984. "Perceptions of Blacks and Hispanics of Two Campus Environments." *Journal of College Student Personnel:* 25: 513–18.

Patterson, Aldrich M., William E. Sedlacek, and William R. Scales. 1984. *The Other Minority: Disabled Student Backgrounds and Attitudes toward Their University and Its Services.* Research Report No. 8-84. College Park: Univ. of Maryland. ED 275 102. 16 pp. MF–01; PC–01.

Pearson, Carol S., Donna L. Shavlik, and Judith G. Touchton, eds. 1989. *Educating the Majority: Women Challenge Tradition in Higher Education.* New York: Macmillan.

Perry, D.C. 1981. "The Disabled Student and College Counseling." *Journal of College Student Personnel* 22: 533–38.

Perry, Floyd, and A.B. Tucher. 1981. "Organizing the Institution to Meet the Needs of Minority and Disadvantaged Students." *College Student Journal* 15(2): 185–89.

Peterson, M.W., R.T. Blackburn, R. Garrison, J. Arce, T. Davenport, and M. Mingle. 1978. *Black Students on White Campuses.* Ann Arbor: Univ. of Michigan, Institute for Social Research. ED 162 601. 388 pp. Not available EDRS.

Pettigrew, T.F. 1985. "New Black-White Patterns: How Best to Conceptualize Them." *Annual Review of Sociology* 11: 329–46.

Pfeffer, Jeffrey. 1983. "Organizational Demography." *Research in Organizational Behavior* 5: 299–357.

———. 1985. "Organizational Demography: Implications for Management." *California Management Review* 28(1): 67–81.

Phillips, W.N., and R.L. Blumberg. 1982. "Tokenism and Organizational Change: Theoretical Examination of an Aspect of Race Relations in Educational Context." Paper presented at a meeting of the American Educational Research Association, April. ED 213 815.

Ponterotto, J.G., I. Grieger, and T.J. Heaphy. 1985. "Students Together against Racial Separation." *Journal of College Student Personnel:* 26(3): 251–53.

Pounds, Augustine W. 1987. "Black Students' Needs on Predominantly White Campuses." In *Responding to the Needs of Today's Minority Students,* edited by D.J. Wright. New Directions for Student Services No. 38. San Francisco: Jossey-Bass.

Quevedo-Garcia, Ennio L. 1987. "Facilitating the Development of Hispanic College Students." In *Responding to the Needs of Today's College Students,* edited by D.J. Wright. New Directions for Student Services No. 38. San Francisco: Jossey-Bass.

Rasor, M. 1981. "EOP and SAA Undergraduates Who Left." Univ. of California–Davis. ED 213 361.

Rendon, Laura, and Amaury Nora. 1987. "Hispanics in the Educational Pipeline." Unpublished paper. Irvine: RAZA Advocates for California Higher Education.

————. 1988. "Hispanic Students." *Educational Record* 68(4)–69(1): 79–85.

Rice, Joy K., and Annette Hemmings. 1988. "Women's Colleges and Women Achievers: An Update." In *Reconstructing the Academy: Women's Education and Women's Studies,* edited by E. Minnich, J. O'Barr, and R. Ronnfield. Chicago: Univ. of Chicago Press.

Richardson, Richard C., Jr., and L.W. Bender 1987. *Fostering Minority Access and Achievement in Higher Education.* San Francisco: Jossey-Bass.

Richardson, Richard C., Jr., and Alfredo de los Santos. 1988. "From Access to Achievement: Fulfilling the Promise." *Review of Higher Education:* 11(4): 323–28.

Richardson, Richard C., Jr., Howard Simmons, and Alfredo de los Santos. 1987. "Graduating Minority Students." *Change* 19(3): 20–22.

Richardson, S.A. 1976. "Attitudes and Behavior toward the Physically Handicapped." *Birth Defects: Original Article Series* 12: 15–34.

Rochin, Refugio, and Adela de la Torres. 1987. "Strengthening Chicano Studies Programs." *La Red/The Net* 1(1): 11–30.

Rokeach, Milton. 1972. *Beliefs, Attitudes, and Values.* San Francsico: Jossey-Bass.

Rooks, Curtiss J. 1988. "How to Keep Ethnic Diversity on the Agenda." Speech given at Career Day, June, Long Beach, California.

Rooney, Glenda D. 1985. "Minority Students' Involvement in Minority Student Organizations: An Exploratory Study." *Journal of College Student Personnel* 26(5): 450–55.

Rossi, Alice. 1987. "Coeducation in a Grades-Stratified Society." In *Educating Men and Women Together,* edited by C. Lasser. Carbondale: Univ. of Illinois.

Roueche, J.E., and G.A. Baker, III. 1987. *Access and Excellence.* Washington, D.C.: Community College Press.

Salganik, Laura H., and Carlyle E. Maw. 1987. "Factors Affecting Hispanics' Participation and Persistence in Postsecondary Education." Paper presented at a meeting of the American Educational Research Association, 20–24 April, Washington, D.C.

Sanders, Danielle. 1987. "Cultural Conflicts: An Important Factor in the Academic Failures of American Indian Students." *Journal of Multicultural Counseling and Development* 15(2): 81–90.

Sandler, Bernice R. 1987. "The Classroom Climate: Still a Chilly One for Women." In *Educating Men and Women Together,* edited by C. Lasser. Carbondale: Univ. of Illinois.

Sandler, Bernice, and R.M. Hall. 1982. *The Classroom Climate: A Chilly One for Women?* Washington, D.C.: Association of American Colleges.

Saslow, R.S. 1981. "A New Student for the Eighties: The Mature Woman." *Educational Horizons* 60(1): 41–61.

Schmidt, Marlin R., and Hazel Z. Sprandel. 1982. *Helping the Learning*

Disabled Student. New Directions for Student Services No. 18. San Francisco: Jossey-Bass.

Sedlacek, William E. 1982. *The Validity and Reliability of a Noncognitive Measure of Nonstudent Retention.* Research Report No. 3-82. College Park: Univ. of Maryland.

——. 1986. "Sources of Method Bias in Test Bias Research." In *Measures in the College Admissions Process.* New York: CEEB.

——. 1987. *Black Students on White Campuses: 20 Years of Research.* Research Report No. 5-87. College Park: Univ. of Maryland.

Sedlacek, William E., and G.C. Brooks, Jr. 1976. *Racism in American Education: A Model for Change.* Chicago: Nelson-Hall.

Sedlacek, William E., and D.W. Webster. 1978. "Admission and Retention of Minority Students in Large Universities." *Journal of College Student Personnel* 19: 242–48.

Seeman, M. 1959. "On the Meaning of Alienation." *American Sociological Review* 24(6): 783–91.

Shavlik, Donna, Judith Touchton, and Carol Pearson. 1989. "The New Agenda of Women for Higher Education." In *Educating the Majority: Women Challenge Tradition in Higher Education,* edited by Carol S. Pearson, Donna L. Shavlik, and Judith G. Touchton. New York: Macmillan.

SHEEO (State Higher Education Executive Officers). 1987. *A Difference of Degrees: State Initiative to Improve Minority Student Achievement.* Research report. Author.

Simmons, Charles E. 1978. "Women's Colleges: A New Agenda." *Educational Record* 59(2): 176–82.

Skinner, Elizabeth Fisk, and R.C. Richardson, Jr. 1988. "Resolving Access/Quality Tensions: Minority Participation and Achievement in Higher Education." Paper presented at a meeting of the Association for the Study of Higher Education, November, St. Louis, Missouri. HE 022 096. 28 pp. MF–01; PC–02.

Slaughter, John B. 1988. "From Isolation to Mainstream: An Institutional Commitment." In *From Survival to Success: Promoting Minority Student Retention,* edited by Melvin C. Terrell and Doris J. Wright. NASPA Monograph Series 9.

Smith, C.H. 1981. "The Predominantly Black College: An Exploration of Its Role and Function." Paper presented at a meeting of the Council on Black American Affairs. ED 207 409. 10 pp. MF–01; PC–01.

Smith, D.H. 1980. *Admission and Retention Problems of Black Students at Predominantly White Universities.* Washington, D.C.: National Advisory Commission on Black Higher Education. ED 201 255. 50 pp. MF–01; PC–02.

Smith, Daryl G. Spring 1982. "The Next Step beyond Student Development: Becoming Partners within Our Institutions." *NASPA Jour-*

nal 19: 53–62.

———. 1983. "Instruction and Outcome in an Undergraduate Setting." In *Studies of College Teaching,* edited by Carolyn Ellner and Carol Barnes. Lexington, Mass.: Lexington Books.

———. 1988. "A Window of Opportunity for Intrainstitutional Collaboration." *NASPA Journal* 26(1): 8–13.

Soldier, N. 1982. "The Adult Learner in Transition: The College Students' Changing Profiles." *Journal of College Admissions* 27(1): 24–26.

Spaights, E., H.E. Dixon, and Susanne Nicholas. 1985. "Racism in Higher Education." *College Student Journal* 19(1): 17–22.

Stampen, Jacob O., and Robert H. Fenske. 1988. "The Impact of Financial Aid on Ethnic Minorities." *Review of Higher Education* 11(4): 337–53.

Stanford Observer. April 1989. Stanford University.

Stern, Joyce D., ed. 1988. *The Condition of Education.* Washington, D.C.: Center for Education Statistics. ED 294 333. 122 pp. MF–01; PC–05.

Stewart, Donald M. 1988. "Overcoming the Barriers to Successful Participation by Minorities." *Review of Higher Education* 11(4): 329–36.

Stilwell, D.N., W.E. Stilwell, and L.C. Perril. 1983. "Barriers in Higher Education for Persons with Handicaps: A Followup." *Journal of College Student Personnel* 24: 337–43.

Stimpson, Catharine. 1987. "New Consciousness, Old Institutions, and the Need for Reconciliation." In *Educating Men and Women Together,* edited by C. Lasser. Urbana: Univ. of Illinois Press.

Stoecker, Judith, Ernest T. Pascarella, and Lee M. Wolfe. 1988. "Persistence in Higher Education: A Nine-Year Test of a Theoretical Model." *Journal of College Student Development* 29: 196–209.

Sudarkasa, Niara. 1987. "Affirmative Action or Affirmation of the Status Quo?" *AAHE Bulletin* 39(6): 3–6.

Sue, Derald Wing. 1979. "Ethnic Identity: The Impact of Two Cultures on the Psychological Development of Asians in America." In *Counseling American Minorities,* edited by D.R. Atkinson, G. Morten, and Derald Wing Sue. Dubuque, Iowa: W.C. Brown.

———. 1981. *Counseling the Culturally Different.* New York: John Wiley & Sons.

———, ed. 1977. "Counseling the Culturally Different." *Personnel and Guidance Journal* 55(7).

Suen, Hoi K. 1983. "Alienation and Attrition of Black Students on a Predominantly White Campus." *Journal of College Student Personnel* 24(2): 117–21.

Suzuki, Robert H. 1984. *Socioeconomic Cultural Pluralism: Its Meaning for the Future and Education.* Proceedings of the Conference on Educational and Societal Futures, 28 April 1983, Anaheim,

California.

Switkin, L.R., and M.D. Gynther. 1974. "Trust, Activism, and Inter-personal Perception in Black and White College Students." *Journal of Social Psychology* 94: 153–54.

Tajfel, H. 1982. "Social Psychology of Intergroup Relations." *Annual Review of Psychology* 33: 1–39.

Terry, Robert. 1981. "The Negative Impact on White Values." In *Impacts of Racism on White America,* edited by B.P. Bowser and R.G. Hunt. Beverly Hills, Cal.: Sage.

Thomas, Gail E. 1981. "The Effects of Standardized Achievement Test Performance and Family Status on Black-White College Access." In *Black Students in Higher Education,* edited by Gail E. Thomas. Westport, Conn.: Greenwood Press.

Tidball, M. Elizabeth. 1973. "Perspective on Academic Women and Affirmative Action." *Educational Record* 54: 130–35.

———. 1976. "Of Men and Research: The Dominant Themes in American Higher Education Include Neither Teaching nor Women." *Journal of Higher Education* 47(4): 373–89.

———. 1980. "Women's Colleges and Women Achievers Revisited." *Signs: Journal of Women in Culture and Society* 5(3): 504–17.

———. 1988. "Women's Colleges and Women Achievers Revisited." In *Reconstructing the Academy: Women's Education and Women's Studies,* edited by E. Minnich, J. O'Barr, and R. Rosenfeld. Chicago: Univ. of Chicago Press.

Tinto, Vincent. 1987. *Leaving College.* Chicago: Univ. of Chicago Press.

Tracey, Terence, and William Sedlacek. 1984. "Noncognitive Variables in Predicting Academic Success by Race." *Measurement and Evaluation in Guidance* 16: 171–78.

———. 1985. "The Relationship of Noncognitive Variables to Academic Success: A Longitudinal Comparison by Race." *Journal of College Student Personnel* 26(5): 405–10.

Trent, William. 1984. "Equity Considerations in Higher Education: Race and Sex Differences in Degree Attainment and Major Field from 1976 through 1981." *American Journal of Education* 92: 280–305.

Trent, William T., and Jomills H. Braddock. 1988. "Trends in Black Enrollment and Degree Attainment." In *Desegregating America's Colleges and Universities,* edited by John B. Williams, III. New York: Teachers College Press.

Turner, Caroline Sotello Viernes. 1987. "Organizational Determinants of the Transfer of Hispanic Students from Two- to Four-Year Colleges." Paper presented at a meeting of the American Educational Research Association, April, Washington, D.C.

Uncapher, B.W., et al. 1983. "Meeting Needs of Adult University Students: A Model Designed by Adult Students." University Park: Pennsylvania State Univ. ED 235 735. 18 pp. MF–01; PC–01.

U.S. Department of Commerce. 1987. *Current Population Reports: Educational Attainment in the U.S., March 1982 to 1985.* Series P- 20, No. 415. Washington, D.C.: Author.

Valencia Community College. 1981. "Staff and Program Development: Black Student Retention, 1980–81." ED 226 773. 24 pp. MF–01; PC–01.

Valverde, L. 1988. "The Missing Element: Hispanics at the Top in Higher Education." *Change* 20(3): 11.

Vasquez, M.J.T. 1982. "Confronting Barriers to the Participation of Mexican-American Women in Higher Education." *Hispanic Journal of Behavioral Sciences* 4(2): 147–65.

Vaz, Kim. 1987. "Building Retention Systems for Talented Minority Students Attending White Universities." *Negro Educational Review* 38(1): 23–29.

Verdugo, R.R. 1986. "Educational Stratification and Hispanics." In *Latino College Students,* edited by M.A. Olivas. New York: Teachers College Press.

Walton, Jean. April 1986. "Can You Really Be Both? Some Thoughts on the Education of Women." *AAHE Bulletin:* 11–15.

Watson, Ann. 1980. "An Analysis of the Concept of Cultural Pluralism." Doctoral dissertation, The Claremont Graduate School.

Webster, D.S. 1984. "Chicano Students in American Higher Education." *Integrated Education* 22(1): 42–51.

Weick, Karl. 1976. "Educational Organizations as Loosely Coupled Systems." *Administrative Science Quarterly* 21(1): 1–19.

———. 1979. *The Social Psychology of Organizing.* New York: Random House.

Weinberg, Meyer. 1982. "In and About the Campus." *Integrated Education* 20(3–5): 3–44.

White, T.J., and William E. Sedlacek. 1987. "White Student Attitudes toward Blacks and Hispanics: Programming Implications." *Journal of Multicultural Counseling and Development* 18(4): 171–83.

WICHE (Western Interstate Commission on Higher Education). 1987. *From Minority to Majority: Education—The Future of the Southwest.* Boulder, Colo.: Author.

Wilkerson, Margaret B. 1987. "How Equal Is Equal Education?: Race, Class, and Gender." In *Educating Men and Women Together: Coeducation in a Changing World,* edited by C. Lasser. Champaign: Univ. of Illinois Press.

———. 1989. "Majority, Minority, and the Numbers Game." In *Educating the Majority: Women Challenge Tradition in Higher Education,* edited by Carol S. Pearson, Donna L. Shavlik, and Judith G. Touchton. New York: Macmillan.

Williams, James H., and Siegmar Muehl. 1978. "Relations among Student and Teacher Perceptions of Behavior." *Journal of Negro Education* 47: 328–36.

Willie, Charles V. 1981. *The Ivory and Ebony Towers: Race Relations and Higher Education.* Lexington, Mass.: Lexington Books.

Willie, Charles V., and Ronald R. Edmonds. 1978. *Black Colleges in America.* New York: Teachers College Press.

Willie, Charles V., and A.S. McCord. 1972. *Black Students at White Colleges.* New York: Praeger Press.

Wilson, K.M. 1980. "The Performance of Minority Students beyond Freshman Year: Testing a 'Late-Bloomer' Hypothesis in One State University Setting." *Research in Higher Education* 13: 23–47.

Wilson, Reginald. 1987a. *Minorities in Higher Education.* Washington, D.C.: American Council on Education. ED 299 844. 45 pp. MF–01; PC–02.

———. 1987b. "Recruitment and Retention of Minority Faculty and Staff." *AAHE Bulletin* 39(6): 11–14.

———. 1988. *Minorities in Higher Education.* Washington, D.C.: American Council on Education.

Women's College Coalition. 1981. *A Study of the Learning Environment at Women's Colleges.* Washington, D.C.: Author.

Wright, Doris J., ed. 1987. *Responding to the Needs of Today's Minority Students.* New Directions for Student Services No. 38. San Francisco: Jossey-Bass.

Wright, Doris J., Anne Butler, Veryl A. Switzer, and Jaculene Gabriel Masters. 1988. "The Future of Minority Retention." In *From Survival to Success,* edited by Melvin C. Terrell and Doris J. Wright. NASPA Monograph Series 9.

Wright, J.J. 1984. "Black Higher Education in the Eighties." *Educational Research* 62(3): 54–57.

Yuker, H.E., J.R. Block, and J.H. Young. 1966. *The Measurement of Attitudes toward Disabled Persons.* Albertson, N.Y.: Human Resources Center.

Zambrana, Ruth E. 1987. "A Profile of Chicana Women in Higher Education: Institutional Barriers." Working paper. Los Angeles: UCLA.

Zuber, P. 1981. "Moral and Ethical Obligations for Colleges and Universities to Minority Students." *Professional Ethics in University Administration.* New Directions for Higher Education No. 33. San Francisco: Jossey-Bass.

INDEX

A

Academic background, 29
Academic integration, 22, 33
Academic preparation, 22, 63
Access
    to education, 16, 63–65
    to facilities, 25, 53
    to information, 27, 33, 48
    to people in power, 51
    to services, 24
Activism, 66
Administrative practices, 75
Admissions criteria, 63–64
Adult students
    campus environment, 24
    enrollment, 11
    growth, 15
    subgroups, 5
African–American students
    access to education, 17, 65
    at white institutions, 20
    by institutional type, 12–13, 14
    campus environment, 21–23
    degree completion, 18, 49
    demographics, 15–16
    distribution by field, 15
    enrollment, 11, 12
    historically African-American colleges, 50–52
    involvement, 43
    males, 31
    persistence factor, 30
    retention rate, 17
    social estrangement, 34
    subgroups, 5
Alienation
    as noninvolvement, 36
    attrition factor, 22
    consistent theme, 1, 19, 44
    definition, 33
    mission/values, 59
American Council on Education, 3
An American Dilemma, 2
American Indians (see Native Americans)
"Americanization," 37
Anglo-Americans: values, 23
Articulation
    K–12, 47, 70–71
    two-year to four-year, 47, 71

R

Racial incidents, 23, 65
Racism
    detriment to learning, 64
    encountering, 22, 23
    ignoring issues of, 5
    naming, 6
Rehabilitation Act of 1973, 24
Ramps, 4, 53
Research
    needs, 69–70
    universities: minority enrollment, 14
Residence halls, 59, 61
Retention
    measure of success, 17–19
    models, 33
Role models
    absence of, 21
    faculty, 56
    token, 44

S

SAT scores
    diversity, 63
    predictor of persistence, 29
Scholarship equity, 62
Scholastic Aptitude Test (see SAT scores)
Section 504/Rehabilitation Act, 24
Selective colleges, 16
Sexism
    detriment to learning, 64
    impact, 6
Sexual harassment, 21, 65
Social factors
    estrangement, 34
    integration, 33
    intergroup relations, 39–41
    isolation, 25, 26
South Americans, 5
Special services
    effect of, 11
    traditional response, 53
Spokespersons, 56
Standardized tests, 62, 64
Stanford University, 62
Stereotypes: breakdown, 42
Stigma: absence of, 47, 53

ASHE-ERIC HIGHER EDUCATION REPORTS

Since 1983, the Association for the Study of Higher Education (ASHE) and the Educational Resources Information Center (ERIC) Clearinghouse on Higher Education, a sponsored project of the School of Education and Human Development at The George Washington University, have cosponsored the *ASHE-ERIC Higher Education Report* series. The 1989 series is the eighteenth overall and the first to be published by the School of Education and Human Development at the George Washington University.

Each monograph is the definitive analysis of a tough higher education problem, based on thorough research of pertinent literature and insitutional experiences. Topics are identified by a national survey. Noted practitioners and scholars are then commissioned to write the reports, with experts providing critical reviews of each manuscript before publication.

Eight monographs (10 before 1985) in the ASHE-ERIC Higher Education Report series are published each year and are available on a individual or subscription basis. Subscription to eight issues is $80.00 annually; $60 to members of AAHE, AIR, or AERA; and $50 to ASHE members. All foreign subscribers must include an additional $10 per series year for postage.

Prices for single copies, including book rate postage, are $15.00 regular and $11.25 for members of AERA, AIR, AAHE, and ASHE ($10.00 regular and $7.50 for members for 1985 to 1987 reports, $7.50 regular and $6.00 for members for 1983 and 1984 reports, $6.50 regular and $5.00 for members for reports published before 1982). All foreign orders must include $1.00 per book for foreign postage. Fast United Parcel Service or first class postage is available for $1.00 per book in the U.S. and $2.50 per book outside the U.S. (orders above $50.00 may substitue 5% of the total invoice amount for domestic postage). Make checks payable to ASHE-ERIC. For VISA and MasterCard payments, include card number, expiration date, and signature. Orders under $25 must be prepaid. Bulk discounts are avilable on order of 15 or more reports (not applicable to subscription orders). Order from the Publications Department, ASHE-ERIC Higher Education Reports, The George Washington University, One Dupont Circle, Suite 630, Washington, DC 20036-1183, or phone us at (202) 296-2597. Write for a complete catalog of all available reports.

1989 ASHE-ERIC Higher Education Reports

1. Making Sense of Administrative Leadership: The 'L' Word in Higher Education
   Estela M. Bensimon, Anna Neumann, and Robert Birnbaum

2. Affirmative Rhetoric, Negative Action: African-American and Hispanic Faculty at Predominantly White Universities
   Valora Washington and William Harvey

---

3. Postsecondary Developmental Programs: A Traditional Agenda with New Imperatives
   Louise M. Tomlinson

4. The Old College Try: Balancing Athletics and Academics in Higher Education
   John R. Thelin and Lawrence L. Wiseman

5. The Challenge of Diversity: Involvement or Alienation in the Academy?
   Daryl G. Smith

1988 ASHE-ERIC Higher Education Reports

1. The Invisible Tapestry: Culture in American Colleges and Universities
   George D. Kuh and Elizabeth J. Whitt

2. Critical Thinking: Theory, Research, Practice, and Possibilities
   Joanne Gainen Kurfiss

3. Developing Academic Programs: The Climate for Innovation
   Daniel T. Seymour

4. Peer Teaching: To Teach is To Learn Twice
   Neal A. Whitman

5. Higher Education and State Governments: Renewed Partnership, Cooperation, or Competition?
   Edward R. Hines

6. Entrepreneurship and Higher Education: Lessons for Colleges, Universities, and Industry
   James S. Fairweather

7. Planning for Microcomputers in Higher Education: Strategies for the Next Generation
   Reynolds Ferrante, John Hayman, Mary Susan Carlson, and Harry Phillips

8. The Challenge for Research in Higher Education: Harmonizing Excellence and Utility
   Alan W. Lindsay and Ruth T. Neumann

1987 ASHE-ERIC Higher Education Reports

1. Incentive Early Retirement Programs for Faculty: Innovative Responses to a Changing Environment
   Jay L. Chronister and Thomas R. Kepple, Jr.

2. Working Effectively with Trustees: Building Cooperative Campus Leadership
   Barbara E. Taylor

3. Formal Recognition of Employer-Sponsored Instruction: Conflict and Collegiality in Postsecondary Education
   Nancy S. Nash and Elizabeth M. Hawthorne

4. Learning Styles: Implications for Improving Educational Practices
   Charles S. Claxton and Patricia H. Murrell

5. Higher Education Leadership: Enhancing Skills through Professional Development Programs
   Sharon A. McDade

6. Higher Education and the Public Trust: Improving Stature in Colleges and Universities
   Richard L. Alfred and Julie Weissman

7. College Student Outcomes Assessment: A Talent Development Perspective
   Maryann Jacobi, Alexander Astin, and Frank Ayala, Jr.

8. Opportunity from Strength: Strategic Planning Clarified with Case Examples
   Robert G. Cope

1986 ASHE-ERIC Higher Education Reports

1. Post-tenure Faculty Evaluation: Threat or Opportunity?
   Christine M. Licata

2. Blue Ribbon Commissions and Higher Education: Changing Academe from the Outside
   Janet R. Johnson and Laurence R. Marcus

3. Responsive Professional Education: Balancing Outcomes and Opportunities
   Joan S. Stark, Malcolm A. Lowther, and Bonnie M.K. Hagerty

4. Increasing Students' Learning: A Faculty Guide to Reducing Stress among Students
   Neal A. Whitman, David C. Spendlove, and Claire H. Clark

5. Student Financial Aid and Women: Equity Dilemma?
   Mary Moran

6. The Master's Degree: Tradition, Diversity, Innovation
   Judith S. Glazer

7. The College, the Constitution, and the Consumer Student: Implications for Policy and Practice
   Robert M. Hendrickson and Annette Gibbs

8. Selecting College and University Personnel: The Quest and the Question
   Richard A. Kaplowitz

1985 ASHE-ERIC Higher Education Reports

1. Flexibility in Academic Staffing: Effective Policies and Practices
   Kenneth P. Mortimer, Marque Bagshaw, and Andrew T. Masland

2. Associations in Action: The Washington, D.C. Higher Education Community
   Harland G. Bloland

3. And on the Seventh Day: Faculty Consulting and Supplemental Income
   Carol M. Boyer and Darrell R. Lewis

4. Faculty Research Performance: Lessons from the Sciences and Social Sciences
   John W. Creswell

5. Academic Program Review: Institutional Approaches, Expectations, and Controversies
   Clifton F. Conrad and Richard F. Wilson

6. Students in Urban Settings: Achieving the Baccalaureate Degree
   Richard C. Richardson, Jr. and Louis W. Bender

7. Serving More Than Students: A Critical Need for College Student Personnel Services
   Peter H. Garland

8. Faculty Participation in Decision Making: Necessity or Luxury?
   Carol E. Floyd

1984 ASHE-ERIC Higher Education Reports

1. Adult Learning: State Policies and Institutional Practices
   K. Patricia Cross and Anne-Marie McCartan

2. Student Stress: Effects and Solutions
   Neal A. Whitman, David C. Spendlove, and Claire H. Clark

3. Part-time Faulty: Higher Education at a Crossroads
   Judith M. Gappa

4. Sex Discrimination Law in Higher Education: The Lessons of the Past Decade
   J. Ralph Lindgren, Patti T. Ota, Perry A. Zirkel, and Nan Van Gieson

5. Faculty Freedoms and Institutional Accountability: Interactions and Conflicts
   Steven G. Olswang and Barbara A. Lee

6. The High Technology Connection: Academic/Industrial Cooperation for Economic Growth
   Lynn G. Johnson

7. Employee Educational Programs: Implications for Industry and Higher Education
   Suzanne W. Morse

8. Academic Libraries: The Changing Knowledge Centers of Colleges and Universities
   Barbara B. Moran

9. Futures Research and the Strategic Planning Process: Implications for Higher Education
   James L. Morrison, William L. Renfro, and Wayne I. Boucher

10. Faculty Workload: Research, Theory, and Interpretation
    Harold E. Yuker

1983 ASHE-ERIC Higher Education Reports

1. The Path to Excellence: Quality Assurance in Higher Education
   Laurence R. Marcus, Anita O. Leone, and Edward D. Goldberg

2. Faculty Recruitment, Retention, and Fair Employment: Obligations and Opportunities
   John S. Waggaman

3. Meeting the Challenges: Developing Faculty Careers*
   Michael C.T. Brooks and Katherine L. German

4. Raising Academic Standards: A Guide to Learning Improvement
   Ruth Talbott Keimig

5. Serving Learners at a Distance: A Guide to Program Practices
   Charles E. Feasley

6. Competence, Admissions, and Articulation: Returning to the Basics in Higher Education
   Jean L. Preer

7. Public Service in Higher Education: Practices and Priorities
   Patricia H. Crosson

8. Academic Employment and Retrenchment: Judicial Review and Administrative Action
   Robert M. Hendrickson and Barbara A. Lee

9. Burnout: The New Academic Disease*
   Winifred Albizu Melendez and Rafael M. de Guzmán

10. Academic Workplace: New Demands, Heightened Tensions
    Ann E. Austin and Zelda F. Gamson

*Out-of-print. Available through EDRS. Call 1-800-227-ERIC.

ORDER FORM

Quantity   **Amount**

_____ Please begin my subscription to the 1989 *ASHE-ERIC Higher Education Reports* at $80.00, 33% off the cover price, starting with Report 1, 1989   _____

_____ Please begin my subscription to the 1990 *ASHE-ERIC Higher Education Reports* at $80.00 starting with Report 1, 1990   _____

_____ Outside the U.S., add $10 per series for postage   _____

Individual reports are avilable at the following prices:

1988 and forward, $15   1983 and 1984, $7.50
1985 to 1987, $10   1982 and back, $6.50

Book rate postage within the U.S. is included. Outside U.S., please add $1 per book for postage. Fast U.P.S. shipping is available within the U.S. at $1 per book; outside the U.S., $2.50 per book; orders over $50 may add 5% of the invoice total. All orders under $25 must be prepaid.

PLEASE SEND ME THE FOLLOWING REPORTS:

Quantity	Report No.	Year	Title	Amount

	Subtotal:	
	Postage(optional):	
	Total Due:	

Please check one of the following:

☐ Check enclosed, payable to GWU-ERIC.
☐ Purchase order attached.
☐ Charge my credit card indicated below:
☐ Visa   ☐ MasterCard

Expiration Date _____

Name _____

Title _____

Institution _____

Address _____

City _____ State _____ Zip _____

Phone _____

Signature _____

SEND ALL ORDERS TO:
ASHE-ERIC Higher Education Reports
The George Washington University
One Dupont Circle, Suite 630
Washington, DC 20036-1183
Phone: (202) 296-2597